Praise for There‍[sa]
The Slave Acro[ss]

"Flores puts a different kind of face on human trafficking in America. She is white, middle-class and blond and looks the epitome of a suburban American woman. She grew up in a wealthy suburb of Detroit in Michigan and did well at school. Yet Flores tells a nightmarish story ..."
— *The London Guardian*, Nov. 22, 2009

"[Theresa Flores] turned her 'hell' into help for other victims"
— *Catholic News Service*, Nov. 16, 2009

"For 20 years, Theresa Flores kept a secret about the tortured life of her teen years"
— *The Today Show*, NBC, February 2009

"I've just finished your book and I want to say thank you—thank you for the courage you brought to the writing, for the truth you spoke so unflinchingly, and for the hope that is your special gift to others. We hear too little from those who have borne slavery. Yet it is this lived experience, and the lessons that come from it, that is our best guide to ending slavery."
— Kevin Bales, Free the Slaves, President, and Author of *Disposable People*

"This is a note of many thanks for coming to Dallas recently and participating in the Women's Symposium; I am still stopped on campus by people who were in attendance and who were deeply moved by your story in particular and by the panel in general."
— Rick Halperin, Southern Methodist University Human Rights Education Program, Director

The Slave Across the Street

The True Story of How an American Teen Survived the World of Human Trafficking

THERESA L. FLORES
with PEGGYSUE WELLS

The Slave Across the Street

The True Story of How an American Teen Survived the World of Human Trafficking

THERESA L. FLORES

with PEGGYSUE WELLS

ampelōn
PUBLISHING
Boise, Idaho
www.ampelonpublishing.com

The Slave Across the Street
Copyright ©2010 by Theresa Flores

ISBN: 978-0-9823286-8-2
Printed in the United States of America
Requests for information should be addressed to:
Ampelon Publishing
PO Box 140675
Boise, ID 83714

Library of Congress Control Number: 2009941479

To order other Ampelon Publishing products, visit us on the web at:
www.ampelonpublishing.com

Cover photography & design: Jared Swafford — SwingFromTheRafters.com

Printed in the United States of America on post-consumer recycled paper

To my amazing children — Samantha, Helena and Trey

To God for giving me strength and to all the people being held in slavery around the world

Table of Contents

Contents

Acknowledgements

First and foremost, I want to honor my family, my three beautiful children for being by my side while I wrote this book. For putting up with my tirades, my emotional breakdowns, and my frustrations while I processed and healed by putting it down on paper. Without them, I would not have had the courage or strength to endure the re-occurring nightmares. Their love gave me hope to get through each day and see a better one the next. They gave me back my smile, my laughter, and a song.

Secondly, I would like to thank my friends and co-workers who supported me while I tackled this seemingly impenetrable mountain. Feeling as if I carried the weight of the world on my shoulders all these years, only to find these precious friends who didn't blink an eye when I told them my story.

Thanks to Mike Bucy, the first person who allowed me to tell my full story. He listened, held me, and offered suggestions for what to do. Although it took years to find another accepting person to hear me, he paved the way for my healing on several different levels. It is only natural that he is employed in one of the caring professions.

Natalie and Brandy were the first to hold my nightmare in their hands. And they still felt proud to know me. Their friendship empowered me to continue my journey until I had completed it. And to Melba, who ministered to me during the writing, helped me process my emotions and pain. She provided foresight to see the extent of my path, giving me strength to travel through the hard part until I could be cleansed again. This time without baths. Until I could smile again. Glow again. In God's glory.

Thanks to God and all His angels for allowing me to stand here today. Alive, healthy, no longer broken, and finally able to tell my story. To help others heal from their wounds. To stop this atrocity from ever happening to another child.

My emotional journey this past year would not have been possible had it not been for the board of Gracehaven. This Christian shelter for domestic minor sex trafficking victims provides a tangible purpose, an outlet, to my mission. During the past year, while helping to develop the shelter and its programs, the board members prayed for me, provided a circle of protection while I shared my story publicly, and comforted me when I felt overwhelmed.

Lastly, thanks to Free the Slaves, Sandy Shepard, Given Kachepa, The Salvation Army, the Central Ohio Coalition to Rescue and Restore, and the Collaborative Initiative Against Human Trafficking in Cleveland Ohio. To all the wonderful catholic nuns in Ohio (Mercy, Dominican, Humility of Mary, and Notre Dame) for their support and eagerness to combat this injustice head on. They listened, never judged or doubted, and covered me with a blanket of love and acceptance. Thanks to the Polaris Project, the National Underground Railroad Freedom Center in Cincinnati, Prevent Child Abuse Ohio and to all the people in Ohio who helped me find my voice, who gave me the determination to finish this book and share my pain to educate others on modern day slavery.

A Note to the Reader

Trafficking in Persons:

"The recruitment, transportation, transfer, harboring or receipt of person, by means of the threat or use of forces or other forms of coercion, of abduction, of fraud, of deception, or the abuse of power or of a position of vulnerability or of the giving or receiving of payments or benefits to achieve consent of a person having control over another person, for the purpose of exploitation."

Exploitation:

"shall include, at a minimum, the exploitation of the prostitution of others or other forms of sexual exploitation"

"The consent of a victim of trafficking in persons to the intended exploitation set forth above, shall be irrelevant where any of the means set forth in the above stated have been used"

"The recruitment, transportation, transfer, harboring or receipt of a child for the purpose of exploitation shall be considered trafficking in persons even if this does not involve any of the means set forth in the above stated"

> – taken from United Nations Convention against
> Transnational Organized Crime, 2000

Lecturing across the United States over the past couple of years, I've told my story a hundred times. While it has been excruciatingly painful, my journey bore fruit in the awareness that my story brings to others.

Whether speaking to five Midwestern Kiwanis men, a small room of retired Catholic nuns in Ohio, an auditorium full of eager and enthusiastic college students in California, Missouri, and Tennessee, or simply speaking privately and candidly to a television journalist who knew nothing of this topic, each time I began with the same question.

"How many of you know about human trafficking?"

A few hands go up.

"Enough to write a paper on it or explain it to someone?"

The hands drop. All but one or two. Time and time again.

While it is disappointing and somewhat alarming that hundreds, even thousands of people know very little about this topic, it is uplifting and encouraging to educate others on human trafficking, how it looks, how it feels, and where it happens.

I recently began a short conversation with another mom at a summer baseball game for our children. She casually asked, "What do you do?"

"I lecture on human trafficking."

"You mean like in India?"

Embracing the opportunity, the teachable moment, I gave this college educated woman, working in the school system, more than she bargained for in the middle of a baseball game. But I was glad for the chance to show her the importance of protecting her teen daughter.

About six months after I put this story on paper and started lecturing on a regular basis, I quickly realized that I hadn't fully described the small details, the circumstances around what happened and the recovery process. When I was originally compelled to write down what happened, it had been painful to dredge up old memories. I felt I was doing good to get it out on paper. My main objective at the time was to simply tell my story, to tell what happened to me so that parents could see how easily this could happen to an average kid from the suburbs.

But each time I spoke, telling a small snippet lasting five minutes to an hour, of the traumatic two years that my story encompasses, the same questions arose over and over again. They needed to be answered.

My desire is that when you close this book, it is not with a sense of horror or sadness for me, but with a clear understanding of how simply and easily this occurs. Right here in the United States. How trafficking seeped into our country. Into our communities. May this project imbue you with a passion to help the child that comes to their mind as they read the book. My desire is that you will share this with other parents. May this book provide hope that a survivor can heal and turn something horrific into a catalyst for good.

As I began working on revisions for this manuscript, I asked my oldest brother to help me make this a more rounded story. After sharing the book with him, we talked about the previous taboo topic, the subject we had avoided for over two decades – those years in Detroit. At last we had permission to ask one another questions, and discover what each of us had endured unbeknownst to the other. Talking it through provided a different perspective and fresh insight that we hadn't been crazy or imagined it all. It was validation.

My brother's contribution brings greater understanding to our family dynamics, my behavior during that time, as well as what my brother, unfortunately, encountered so the traffickers could ensure I remained in my position of indebtedness.

I also wanted to include the perspective of the person I first successfully shared my story with in college. The first successful relationship I had that helped me heal and trust again. This healing was especially important from the further wounds of unknowing strangers, unbelievers that this could truly be 'slavery,' comments and opinions that I must have had an option, therefore it could not be slavery. I suppose I was seeking validation again. Embedded deep within our soul, rejection and shame are emotions that people with post traumatic syndrome disorder (PTSD) live with daily. I needed another person's perspective on how this trauma changed me, the psychological and physical aftermath of what it did to me. Both internally and externally.

I realize that this is a difficult subject for many to embrace, and that no amount of witnesses or perspectives I provide will convince some people that I had no other viable options in the circumstances. It is my greatest hope that people will understand the most important message in my story is the sexual exploitation of a child.

The victim is a child.

A child who *feels* there are no options.

This is *my* story of a girl from the suburbs who was manipulated, coerced, and threatened into terrible things against her will, while others profited. Since speaking publicly, others have confessed similar, sad stories. It is not important for the nonbeliever to acknowledge the truth of what happened to me. What is important is that people become aware that this is happening in the United States, in cities, and in small towns. To kids of every color, every socio-economic background, with two parents, or no parents. It is vital that people understand how simply this can happen to *any* child.

Preface

This book took many years to write. The abuse lasted for two long years, a small fraction of time in relation to my forty-something years. Yet nightmares can last an eternity, affecting the psyche and soul.

Years passed between being brave enough to write each chapter. I cracked open Pandora's Box, only to slam it shut again each time. I was afraid to pry it open, exposing my deepest and darkest secrets, one at a time. I finally gained the spiritual strength I needed to peek in once more and confront my inner demons head on. This time for the sake of healing others.

I completed the book as part of my healing. The trauma no longer holds me captive, as I was nearly 26 years ago.

The growing question as I wrote the book was not the title, but what to name the traumatic *experience*. As humans, we like – require – a one- or two-word label that sums up everything we need to know about one's personality, medical/mental condition, race/ethnicity, religion, education, and political views. I struggled to find this much needed label for what I had experienced. I couldn't accurately finish the book without it. I needed to know the term for myself.

After I escaped the heinous abuse, I miraculously resumed a normal teenage life. On the outside anyway. Hidden hundreds of miles from my abusers, I graduated high school and then went away to college. Sexuality and promiscuity surrounded college life, used as an expression of freedom and experimentation. My world spun out of control. I lacked the emotional strength and successful past experiences with saying no. Without this power, many victims of sexual abuse deal with their past by either turning completely away from any sexual activity or become overtly sexual. I needed help.

During my junior year of college, I revealed my story to someone I was dating. I had shared my past only once before with disastrous results. It wasn't relevant to the person that I had been a child while a knife was held to my throat. He felt that I should have been strong, said no, and not let it happen.

This time was different. It was the first healthy relationship I had experienced, so I let down my guard once again. He listened, let me cry, and calmly advised me to seek counseling and the police. I took his advice and called the police who quickly turned me away, saying the statute of limitations was over for rape. Sadly, these officials did not recognize signs of trafficking, nor inquire if I had been a minor during the exploitation.

Next, I went to the Rape Crisis Center on campus and told my story to a stranger. Shocked into silence, the stunned professional was unprepared for my story. It was a reaction I've faced many times since. The counselor recommended a group session for rape victims.

I sat there, while the other girls in the group went around the circle and shared their story. One by one, each woman described the incident they experienced. Then it was my turn. All eyes fell upon me, the new girl. How could I describe in one to two sentences and in under two minutes, what had happened to me? I'd not processed the horror successfully, nor received a positive, supportive reaction to my story.

I simply couldn't share. I stood and walked out, never to return. My story didn't fit the parameters. Yes, I was raped. Yes, I was gang raped, attacked, and left for dead. But that was only part of my story. That merely scratched the surface. My experience went much further than that. It wasn't once, wasn't twice, but lasted for years. Against my will. To pay back a debt. For the benefit and profit of others.

It would take another 21 years to find the label I desperately sought. To find support from those who had already heard stories similar to mine. To receive understanding rather than damnation, questioning, or unbelieving looks.

I didn't look like the typical person this sort of thing happened to. I didn't fit the mold, if there was one. It took from the time I was 15 years old until I was 41 to see those kind eyes, and receive that warm hug from an understanding stranger. To find my label. Find my truth. To come to terms with the reality that I was a white, upper-middle class teenager. A budding track star. An all-American, Catholic girl. And a victim of human trafficking.

I wasn't a runaway. I wasn't abused at home. I had professional parents, loving siblings, and a privileged lifestyle. Yet I had been a victim of *human trafficking*. I had been commercially, sexually exploited as a child. I had been a teenage sex slave in the United States.

Introduction

Lying in the bathtub, I knew it was time. Time to pour out the past onto paper. As I pondered this thought, I wondered what would happen, not *if*, but *when*, I finally opened Pandora's Box and wrote my story for others to read.

This bath was different from the other baths. It was a turning point. Even though I would expose my naked self, my soul, I would finally be whole. Finally be cleansed. Washed free of these years of sin and guilt. Of the secrets and the what-ifs.

Like a soft womb, the fragrant, warm water embraced and soothed me. After long years locked within the dark corners of my mind, the memories slowly seeped out. I had kept them contained, afraid that if I allowed myself to remember, my fragile state of mind might crack.

I prided myself on being a strong woman. I had endured more than most people could ever fathom. After all, I had survived my own nightmare, hadn't I? But that was physical. This was mental. One can never guarantee how strong the psyche really is. Or what the results will be.

Was I strong enough now? Had I healed enough to go down this path? To remember what I had endured? To press myself to remember the parts I had blocked to protect myself? Could I face the silent horrors which no one knew about?

Baths have always been a symbolic experience. Almost surreal. Most women enjoy baths. They soak in the warm, sudsy, scented waters. Soak away the craziness of the day, the responsibilities and chaos. Baths give permission to unwind. Relaxing, peaceful, tranquil, medicinal.

Baths represent much more than relaxing or cleansing our bodies. Our first breath is taken as we emerge from the uterine bag of water in which we developed and lived for our first months of existence. Next we are washed clean and presented to our parents, to the world. Parents document their child's first bath as momentous. Many receive the waters of baptism to symbolically cleanse us of sin, proclaiming our commitment to be followers of Christ. At death, many receive final rites, a blessing of holy water by a priest.

Baths – water, not only cleanse us but also mark important events in our lives. They cleanse our souls and make us new again. They heal us and nourish our soul. Our body requires water in order to survive.

Taking a bath has always been important to me. Baths allowed me to think deeply and have a good cry, which no one could hear while the hot water gushed from the faucet. Baths permitted me an opportunity for soul searching and at times, provided me with answers to my questions.

I took baths for another important reason. They were taken with an earnest wish of washing away sins and regrets. My regrets and the sins of others. But this never seemed to happen. Baths were taken as a cleansing ritual, to start a new beginning, a rebirth. With fresh, clean water. Yet the dirty feeling still remained, even after exiting the waters.

For all these years, I have carried the burden of what happened before and after that memorable bath when I was 15-years-old.

I.

They Don't Know My Name

To the men who used me night after night, I was not a human being. As they performed the most intimate act a man and a woman engage in, I was only a dollar value. A commodity. To know this in my formative teenage years, during the period when a woman defines her worth and identity, proved devastating. How does a child begin to process this? To feel and hear that so many, many men didn't care about me at all, in fact they celebrated my humiliation, degradation and pain, that was a critical wound to my soul. It was a bitter view of inhumanity to an idealistic teenager.

This awareness leads a victim of human trafficking to lose all love, even for themselves. When others don't value or love you, it becomes difficult to love yourself. There is no healthy example. Shame, embarrassment, and guilt fill the vacuum where love should thrive.

Often the heart and the brain give conflicting messages. My heart was wounded from so many men treating me without care or value. Certain locations, smells, words and songs can trigger memories. One day a friend and I watched a movie on trafficking called *Call and Response*. As I sat in my theatre seat, trying to be strong and not remember, the passionate words of a song penetrated my carefully constructed shell.

"They don't know my name..."

The memory rushed forward like a wave crashing upon a rocky beach. On that night the room smelled of sex, smoke, and musky incense when an older, attractive, olive skinned man entered. He looked upon me, splayed naked on the bed, my hair rumpled, my young body wet and exhausted from being mounted by so many men. Rarely did anyone look me in the eyes but this man did and I saw admiration and sadness reflected there.

"What is your name?" he asked in a rough accent.

Knowing I would be punished, I didn't dare say a word.

The kind-eyed man seemed out of place among these other brutes.

He turned to Nick. "What is her name?"

Nick looked at him with disgust. "What does it matter? She has no name."

His words struck my heart. I turned my head to the side as tears rolled down my cheek.

"Never mind," I heard the man say. "I have changed my mind. The deal is off."

I turned to watch the dignified man walk regally out of the room.

I felt Nick's anger and his repulsion of the man who refused his prize. "Get up and get dressed," he spat. "You're no good to me anymore tonight. Get out of here. I will tell Daniel to take you home now. And this better not ever happen again! You are costing me money!"

While I was grateful that I didn't have to endure any more that night, all I could think of was that this kind man hadn't helped me escape.

I was worth nothing.

I didn't matter.

I had no name.

The Beginning

Lukewarm water is filling the tub. It is a bathroom foreign to me, not in my own house. The sound of the flow of water exiting the faucet and streaming steadily into the tub is hypnotizing. I feel alien, as if I am outside of my body looking down upon myself. I see a young, naked girl. She is crying softly, careful to do as she has been instructed and not make a sound. Her body shakes with tremors, rampant emotions flood her as the water rises over her body.

Fear of being discovered, *shame* of what has just occurred and *anger* of what can not be undone. Bright red blood circles the water, floating around her privates. A young man walks into the bathroom and I unwillingly float back into my body.

"I am sorry, Theresa. I didn't know. You should have told me."

I stare at him as tears run down my face. As the blood pools in between my legs. "I did," I choke out and cry harder.

"Shhhh," he insists. "My family is downstairs. I don't want them to hear. I don't want them to know you are here."

Fear sets in again. I am not the only female in the strange house. Alone with a young man. But I am a foreigner.

"Get changed and I will take you home," Daniel says.

Like he is doing me a favor. I oblige and gingerly dry my sore body. Numb and dazed, I change back into my high school track uniform.

"I have to get you out of here without my mother or aunts seeing you," Daniel cautions.

There wasn't anyone in the house when I got here a few hours earlier. But time has stopped for me. It stopped hours before. When I was raped.

3.
The Move

In those days, it was considered a mixed marriage. Mom was from a large, Irish Catholic family. My father was a WASP, commonly known back then as a White, Anglo-Saxon, Protestant. Though this caused a minimal amount of conflict inside the family and at various parishes we belonged to, in general, it wasn't a big deal.

My parents raised me and my three younger brothers to believe in family, stressed the importance of hard work and to always do the right thing. For the most part, we siblings are close. We were fortunate that our mother was able to stay at home with us while growing up, which was the norm in those days. She rarely worked outside the home except on the rare occasions when we needed extra money for braces, college, or a trip to Ireland for herself and my grandmother.

It was my duty as a female child to help care for the family and it was expected that someday I would have a family of my own. Chores were divided by gender and my jobs were to clean the inside of the house, which included the bathrooms, sweeping, and dusting. My brothers were in charge of the outside chores, including mowing the lawn, raking, taking out the trash, and shoveling snow.

Sometimes I negotiated a trade. Riding the lawn mower while listening to music on headphones and getting a suntan, I wondered how this could possibly be considered a chore. I never liked or understood the division of chores by our gender, but it was consistent and predictable.

My family was goal-oriented and competitive. Most of the extended family members attended college, worked hard, and had successful lives. It was assumed that I would go to college. The only questions permitted were which school I would attend and what would be my major. Many things were expected of my brothers and myself, as is typical in the upper middle class socioeconomic group. We were children of parents who had been raised with everything yet struggled for their own success.

My father was a top executive for a large company. It was the era of large companies and great deals of money. Success and maintaining our lifestyle required constantly accepting promotions and transfers. We moved every two years. By the time I was 18 years old, I had attended three high schools in four years, lived in four states, and moved ten times.

Knowing we faced another move, one summer my parents took us camping with long-time family friends and we spent a day on a friend's yacht at a popular lake island retreat. I met my boyfriend on Lake Erie at Put-In-Bay, Ohio. Jim was two years older than me and my first real boyfriend. He lived several hours away in a suburb of Cleveland, Ohio, and we wrote letters and talked on the phone daily.

Jim and I had big dreams. Our new, young love knew no limits. It was innocent, love at first sight and nothing could bring us down. Not even distance. We planned to go to prom together and planned one day to get married. Both from Catholic families, we had seriously discussed and agreed not to have sex until we married.

Though he lived several hours away and didn't have a car, my parents didn't like that Jimmy was older. They strongly recommended that it would be best for me if I dated other boys. I, of course, balked at this but as the dutiful daughter, agreed for agreeing sake.

I was a freshman in high school when my dad announced we were moving.

"Again?"

"I don't want to leave my friends," my brother protested.

"I know," mom said. "We're all leaving friends."

"I was just starting to fit in," I added.

"I'm tired of moving," my brother complained.

"We're all tired of moving," mom agreed.

"How many times have we moved?" another brother wanted to know.

"This is number eight for me," I said.

"This will be the last time," mom promised.

"That's what you and dad said last time."

Each move, it grew harder to make friends but it was also a chance to make a fresh start if I had screwed things up in the last place. This time we moved into an affluent neighborhood in Birmingham, Michigan, a suburb of Detroit.

In the 1980's Detroit was huge, dangerous, thrilling, and exciting. On weekend trips with my mother to the farmers' market, I explored the city. Growing up with Midwest farming relatives, I was used to seeing bushel baskets overflowing with fresh picked green beans, plump tomatoes, and glossy green peppers. This place was different. Vendors hawked unidentifiable fruits and vegetables from all over the globe. Vast warehouses overflowed with foreign cheeses and teas, scenting the air and enticing me inside every time we visited the market. There were spices and smells even my cultured and worldly mother didn't have a name for.

Dead chickens hung upside down with all their body parts still attached, or a shopper could go around to the back of a building and select a live bird, still clucking, to be slaughtered and cleaned while the shopper waited.

In this city, a diverse mixture of cultures lived amongst one another. Some groups mixed together in one neighborhood, others divided by unseen street lines. Detroit and its suburbs were dark and dingy one minute, and abundantly rich the next. We had moved to the Beverly Hills of the area. Our town bordered Southfield and half of the kids from this town attended my school.

Just one street separated Birmingham from Southfield, yet the average house in Southfield was valued at $155,000 and whites made up 38 percent of the population. For the first time, I wasn't in the majority, nor was I one of the richest kids in town. The kids I went to school with consisted of a "significantly high percentage, above the states average, of foreign born people."

This fact would change the rest of my life.

4.
Adjusting

Making friends in my new school was difficult. I was older and it wasn't the same as starting third grade when everyone wanted to befriend the new kid.

This place was different. A big city with communities from Irish, German, Italian, and Polish immigrant groups. The strong influence of Jewish, Muslim, and Arabic ethnic groups was foreign to me.

My mother thrived in our new home. She embraced the cultures. We attended ethnic festivals downtown, sampled unusual selections of food, sat on the cement steps of the outdoor theatre and listened to the cultural music of the week. Proud people wore the costumes of their native country and danced as if it were a hundred years ago. Mom opened our home to cultural exchange students from other countries, giving them a bed and family to live with while studying in the United States. Eventually she took a position with the local exchange student chapter to help find families for students coming here from various countries.

Mom joined The Gourmet Club. Monthly, a group of four couples decided upon a country as the focus of their gourmet dinner. The women discussed the menu, one couple provided the main course, another researched the music, drinks, and decorations. An adult-only occasion, my dad was an eager participant.

Though my brothers and I were enlisted to help peel 20 pounds of shrimp, or help in the preparation of their meal, we didn't complain much. We were used to being shooed to our rooms while our parents' adult friends came over. We made our own party of it with Bugles (a big treat), soda, and samplings from the dinner they were making. We spent the evening watching the *Wizard of Oz* or *Chitty Chitty Bang Bang*. Sometimes I told stories to my brothers.

When the party went on late into the night and my brothers got bored, they made tents out of bed sheets nailed to the walls. Heads hurting from a long night of partying, our parents wouldn't check on us until late the following morning. By that time, I had cleaned up our mess, making sure not to anger them.

Mom's other endeavor in our new home was Birmingham's community theatre. She auditioned in the small playhouse and rehearsed upcoming roles. She was good. While my father was away on business, it gave her something to do.

Life then wasn't like it is today. Children weren't into multiple sports; our parents didn't shuttle us to games and practices. We didn't sit around the kitchen table doing our homework together. Each of us chose one activity, usually scouts, and rode our bike if we wanted to go somewhere. Mom wasn't about to take us to the mall just because we were bored and begged.

I went lots of places alone. The park, the private swim club we belonged to, the fast food restaurant at the corner, and the library. I adapted to the new town and the new way of life as best as I could. My grades in school were average. I didn't excel at anything in particular. I was pretty, but not beautiful. Average sized, but not skinny. I was in choir but didn't have solos. Because I was lonely, making new friends and being accepted was extremely important to me.

Dad's job required a great deal of entertaining in our home and in public. I was subtly taught to be well behaved when others, particularly dad's co-workers and sales clients were around. I could carry on a conversation with adults on a multitude of topics. I didn't know in-depth amounts of a particular subject but just enough to hold an intelligent conversation.

My grandfather was a well-known, successful attorney and it was not uncommon for me to visit a judge's home for dinner, fly in airplanes with politicians, and go to parties with Bishops and celebrities. My family's success was dependent on my behavior, reputation, and the importance of me doing as I was instructed. It was an unstated societal rule for the upper class that as a child, I must not embarrass my parents.

****

Grove High School's homecoming dance was in October. It was my first dance at my new school.

"Will you go to the dance with me?" He was a nice, quiet, Jewish boy, somewhat distant and shy, but I was happy to have a date to the semi-formal occasion and fit in for a change. In a two-piece dress of purple and lace, I was pretty as a picture. A picture of us dancing even appeared in that year's yearbook. Though I don't think we ever spoke again after the dance, we exchanged smiles as we passed each other in the school halls.

I made a few friends and on weekends we went to the high school football games and movies, had sleepovers, and frequently went to Farrell's for ice cream. Sometimes I felt the kids were letting me hang out with them, as if they were doing me a favor. They accepted another girl the year before who was a military brat. No one really liked her but I suppose they figured if they let her in, they should let me in as well. Regardless of the reason, I was determined to make the best of it, as I had done so many other times. Until we would be told to pack up the boxes again and move to the next place.

5.
Different Kinds of Kids

The majority of the high school population consisted of Jewish kids with a large percentage of Chaldeans (Catholic Arabs), and a few Muslim Arabs. On my first day of school I was stunned to see a security guard posted at the end of the school hallway. I had never even talked to a policeman, let alone had one in my school. My only exposure to schools with police, security systems, and metal detectors was from stories of inner city schools in movies and on television.

Though the other students didn't seem phased, I didn't understand why a guard would be in a school for children. I had attended schools in rural areas of Michigan and southern Indiana where classes basically shut down during the fall months because nearly 80 percent of the boys were hunting with their fathers. In Birmingham, the school closed on Jewish holidays.

I was accepted into the "B" group of kids. The average kids. The second tier to the popular kids. Military brats and other kids who moved around were rarely permitted into the popular group. Slender and well-developed for my age with strawberry blond hair highlighted from many perms and time in the sun, I was pretty but not stunning enough for the "A" group. My clothing was another reason I wasn't permitted into the popular clique.

As the oldest daughter with three younger brothers, I had a great deal of responsibility. I received a modest allowance for certain approved purchases. Mom didn't approve of name brand clothing nor did she approve of another person's name appearing on my body, so designer labels or make-up was out of the question. Calvin Klein and Gloria Vanderbilt were the rage, while I wore ragged, no-name clothes.

Household rules dictated that I not shave my legs or date until I was 16. What would happen to me before my 16th birthday would make all the rules ridiculous and absurd.

6.

A New Culture

I was drawn to the Arab culture, prevalent in my school and community. The more I learned about it, the more intrigued I became. This was a culture of people thrown out of their country years before due to religious persecution.[i] Chaldeans are a minority within the Iraqi population due to their religion, Christianity.[ii] Iraqi Christians compose a mere three to six percent of the population in Iraq.[iii] They came to the United States from a country once called Chaldea, presently known as Iraq.[iv] Arabic in ethnicity, yet of the Christian religion, they practice the Catholic faith. While living in Iraq and the surrounding predominantly Muslim countries, Chaldeans were forced to leave their country in order to survive and keep their Catholic faith.

Chaldeans immigrated to the U.S. in the early 1900's, encouraged by Middle Eastern immigrants already here.[v] Michigan became a location of choice for Chaldean immigrants because it was one of the few states that still permitted first cousins to marry one another.[vi] Marrying within the family network is common, if not expected.

Most of the students I went to school with were first generation American born, yet some of the older students had slight accents when they spoke. They spoke Arabic at home and English at school. Fascinated, I wanted to befriend this group. I thought we had a great deal in common. First, we were both Catholic. Though some had their own Chaldean Catholic churches, many attended the same church as I did. Also, similar to my Irish ethnicity, both of us had strong family ties.

But that is where the similarities ended. In my Irish heritage, the people are mostly fair skinned and light eyed. Material items aren't generally of value, and women and men are equal partners in life. The Chaldean culture was scary yet exciting. Females stayed to themselves. Chaldean families followed strict traditional roles differentiated by strict gender lines.[vii] Girls were safe in their own groups at school and at church. They didn't get involved in after school activities, going straight home after school each day. Closely watched by the male Chaldeans, mostly relatives, the girls were secluded, quiet, and demure.

I was immediately drawn to a handsome, young Chaldean boy named Daniel. In the same grade as me, he seemed several years older. He had jet black hair, dark eyes, olive skin, and a beautiful smile. He dressed impeccably in crisply pressed Ralph Lauren shirts and slacks. He wore gold jewelry, which was typical of most Arabs in my school. He smelled wonderful.

Daniel worked part-time in the school's student store. Every time I noticed he was working, I'd go in and buy an eraser or a pencil. He was attentive when I was around. I knew he was attracted to my blonde hair, creamy white skin, and my feisty spirit. My girlfriends warned me against him.

"You're off limits," they told me. "You aren't Chaldean. He could never date you. Don't even think about it." I didn't listen.

My family valued culture and diversity. My grandfather assisted immigrants with legal problems and my parents sponsored international students who lived with us from time to time. My boyfriend, Jimmy, was Italian-American. I had attended several school dances with Jewish boys.

In my previous schools, boys tolerated girls and teased them. Most of the guys were heavily involved in sports, outdoor activities like four wheeling, skating, and racing. They helped their dads on the farm or at work. Young good ole' boys in the making. It was different in Birmingham where the boys were suave, well dressed, and smelled good. They passed me in the halls, scanned me over, smiling, enticing. These boys didn't know what it was like to work outside in the cold or go hunting. Their fathers owned their own stores or businesses. They were making money and taking everything from life that they could.

The attraction between Daniel and me grew stronger each day. I liked him for his differences. He was exotic. I suppose he liked me too, though at the time I wasn't sure. In addition to the physical attraction, an air of being off limits to one another added excitement.

In Daniel's culture, women were a lower status. Young men were taught not to respect women. Or take no for an answer.

7.
Spring Semester

By the spring semester, I struggled with my grades. The district's strict academic standards were different from rural settings where teachers were glad you showed up and hoped you were wearing shoes.

Daniel and I continued eyeing each other while boys in my own league pursued me. Jim and I wrote letters and planned my upcoming birthday and his prom in the spring. We had a competition writing letters—he would write five pages to me one day and I would write six back. Then he would write seven. For Valentine's Day, he sent me a four-foot tall Hallmark card. I was shocked when the mailman delivered it and happy for the attention and love I received from him on a daily basis. From different socio-economic groups, two different ways of life, we saw the similarities in each other, not the differences.

Mom took me to a mall in Saginaw to shop for my prom dress. I selected a baby blue floor length satin gown with white, sheer lace. She also bought a baby blue satin suit with pants and vest. It was the first chic, stylish clothes I owned. My parents let me plan my sweet 16 birthday party. It would be a great party in our recently refinished basement. Now, I would definitely fit into the group.

In February, the high school announced tryouts for the track team. I had been on the track team at my previous school and surprisingly found that I wasn't half bad. We practiced after school every day, doing drills in the gym due to the frigid Michigan weather. I dreaded conditioning but liked being part of the team. I had more freedom, staying after school every day and going home later in the afternoon.

In speech class, two boys sat behind me. Bassim and Hassam spoke broken English with strong accents. Dressed in simple clothing, without cologne, and wearing small gold jewelry, they weren't the same as the other Chaldean boys. Cousins from a lower-middle class family, they were considered black sheep. Passing back their graded papers, I knew they were having difficulty in class and I befriended them.

8.
The Phone Call

My long conversations with Jim tied up the home phone for hours and my mom did not like that she couldn't receive calls. The perk when we moved again was that each of us had our own private line in our bedrooms.

Late one evening, I was watching television with my family, when the phone rang on the main house line. My mom went to answer it and returned with a scowl on her face.

"Theresa, phone," she said. "Get rid of those Arabs right now."

Confused, I went to the nearest phone in the hall. "Hello?"

"Theresa, this is Daniel, from school. I work in the school store."

Like I didn't know who he was.

"Yes?"

"Look, I need to talk you…"

My mom was standing next to me. "Get rid of them, Theresa," she repeated. "Right now!"

"But he's from school. He has a question about homework," I lied. I was flattered that he called me. I heard other voices in the background.

"Theresa. How's it going baby?" I couldn't place this unfamiliar voice on the line. But I could see my mom getting angry.

"I gotta go," I hurriedly said. "Bye."

My mom took the receiver and slammed it down. "We don't accept calls from Arabs at this house," she stated firmly.

"They aren't Arabs, mom," I responded. "They're Chaldeans."

"I don't care who they are. They won't be calling here anymore, do you understand?"

I nodded. Her reaction seemed unusual for her. All I could think about was that Daniel had called me. *How did he get my number?* It didn't matter, he had called me.

The next day at school, it was hard not to tell my friends that Daniel, the gorgeous Chaldean, had called me at home. But I kept it to myself, going from class to class with a smile on my face. Approaching the cafeteria at lunch, I realized I had left my lunch in my locker.

"Hey, guys, I gotta run back to my locker," I told my friends. "I'll be right back."

I walked to the opposite end of the high school, past the security guard who was perched on his stool reading a book, turned the corner and headed to my locker. Concentrating on the locker combination, I didn't hear anyone approach. As I found the last number of the combination and pulled open my locker, a hand reached up and slammed my locker door shut.

"Hello there, Theresa."

It was Daniel's two cousins. *What were their names?*

"Hi," I said tentatively, feeling fear.

"Do you know why we are here?"

"I have no idea."

They laughed eerily. Chills ran up my spine. With one hand resting on my closed locker door, he leaned dangerously close, his face just inches from mine. "You hung up on us last night. We don't like when people hang up on us."

"I wasn't talking to you. Daniel called me. My mom hung up the phone because I am not allowed to talk to boys."

"Well, you hung up on us," the older, quiet one accused.

"No," I insisted, not knowing why I was trying to convince them. "I said good-bye before I got off. It wasn't my fault. It was my mother."

The shorter, stouter cousin closed the gap between us and stood inches away from me. The second cousin backed me against my locker. "Don't ever hang up on us again."

As I nodded, he spit in my face. Saliva covered my eyes and forehead, and ran down my face, over my nose, my mouth, and chin. They walked away, laughing.

Shaking, I wiped the thick spit from my face and tried to compose myself. I was afraid that someone had witnessed this humiliation. The halls were usually a busy place. Now they were oddly empty. I forgot about my lunch, walked passed the policeman who had done nothing. He kept his eyes down, pretending to read his book. Pretending he hadn't seen what had just occurred.

When I returned to the cafeteria, lunch was nearly over.

"Where have you been, Theresa," my friend asked.

"I was in the bathroom. I don't feel so good all of a sudden. I'm going to call my mom and go home sick."

At home, I told my mom I had cramps and ran water in the bathtub. I eased into the warm soothing waters. I had been violated and felt dirty. Spit upon.

9.
Changed Forever

As spring approached, my parents said I could invite anyone to my upcoming 16th birthday party. Even boys. I desperately wanted Jim to come from Cleveland but we were planning to go to his prom in May and he couldn't afford a bus ticket for my birthday party in addition to the prom expenses. I tried to understand, but I was disappointed. My friends were beginning to wonder if he was real.

I secretly had a crush on Daniel. I invited him and ten other friends. My friends didn't approve of me inviting Daniel but I didn't care. I was going to be a woman, be allowed to finally date, shave my legs, and wear make-up without hiding it anymore. All my dreams would come true when I turned 16.

On a cold February day, after school, I rushed to the gym locker room to change into my track uniform for practice. Waiting for the other girls to show up, I realized I had forgotten some books in my locker. I ran down the hall, using it as an excuse to warm up. As I turned the corner, I was amazed to see Daniel. *Who else's locker was near mine? Who could he be looking for? Surely not me.*

"Do you want a ride home?" he asked.

"Sure, practice just got cancelled," I lied. "I just need to get my coat."

Anything to get to spend time with him without the watchful eyes of my disapproving friends. I went by the gym, grabbed my things and told the coach that I didn't feel well all of a sudden and was going to go home. Daniel and I walked to the school parking lot to his new black Pontiac Trans Am GT. It was an expensive, sporty car and I hurried to get inside so my running mates wouldn't see me leaving practice with him.

Daniel drove down the street and turned the wrong way. I lived within walking distance to the school in the other direction.

"I live the other way," I told him.

Daniel gave me a beautiful smile. "I know, Theresa. But I want to spend some time with you and get to know you better. I have wanted to do this for a long time. But I need to run by my house first to get something. I'll take you home after that."

How could I say no? Here was the guy I had had a crush on all year long and he wanted to spend time with me. I was too naive to be scared.

Daniel pulled into the driveway of a huge house. There were no other cars in the driveway and alarms went off in my head. *But I trust him*, I justified. I thought I knew him. After all, I had a boyfriend and was getting married when I graduated. Daniel and I had stolen moments to talk. Little chats in the hall, at my locker, and in the store. He had asked me if I had a boyfriend and I had hesitantly told him yes. We attended the same Catholic church, though more often it was his sisters and female family members who came. He was Catholic and I assumed that he knew I carried the same values and morals stressed in the church teachings. I ignored the red flags.

"I need to run inside," he said. "Do you want to come with me?"

I looked around. I didn't want to sit and wait in the car and I was interested in seeing the inside of this foreigner's home. It looked like it could house many families. Again I ignored the red flags.

Inside, Daniel showed me around the house.

"Where is everyone?" I asked. I was used to my mother and brothers being home when I got back from school every day.

"Don't know," he hedged. "They should be home any minute, though."

Dark and mysterious, the house was stunningly decorated. Rich colored rugs hung everywhere. Gold framed pictures and candlesticks were in excess. It smelled like incense at Mass on holy days.

Following him upstairs, more warning alarms sounded in my head. "We should get going, Daniel. My mother will be expecting me," I said, lying again. She thought that I was where I was supposed to be, at track practice. Not for a moment would she be sitting at home thinking I was with this cute Chaldean guy in his family's home. If I couldn't talk to him on the phone, I knew I would never be permitted to go to his house.

"Just a few minutes, Theresa. I want to spend some time with you," he pleaded. "You like me don't you? I have always liked you a lot."

I knew better. But his sweet voice coupled with my desire to be special to him lured me into staying. From the mini refrigerator in his bedroom, he pulled out a soda. With his back to me, he poured the liquid into a glass and handed it to me. It tasted strange. Bitter. Perhaps it was the odd smells of the house, the incense, or maybe the soap they used to wash the glasses.

We sat on his bed and my heart sped up with the knowledge that he was going to kiss me. I was feeling dizzy, not sure if it was because I was so excited at the thought of him kissing me or if I was getting sick. I had day-dreamed of this moment for a long time. I thought of Jimmy. But I knew a kiss was harmless. After all, I was young and my parents said they wanted me to date others before I settled down with one guy.

Daniel kissed me. He was older and experienced. I was 15 years old and a virgin. But I was lonely for attention, to be accepted and loved by someone close to me. We kissed for a long time. Then things began to progress. I had had more experience in petting than I cared to admit, but I always knew when to stop the boys. I enjoyed the attention boys gave me, but I was a good Catholic girl and knew when to call it quits.

My head reeled under Daniel's caresses. Or could it have been from the soda? Daniel's hands began roaming, distracting me as he tugged my track shorts down to my knees. Alarms sounded anew in my brain and I knew I had to tell him to stop. I knew *right* where that line was.

"I want you now." His voice was muffled against my flesh, his hands insistent.

"No, Daniel! You have to stop now! I need to go home."

Daniel ignored my wishes.

"Daniel! I mean it. I have to go. My mother will be worried about me," I pleaded.

Still not even an acknowledgement from Daniel. Panic crowded my throat. No one had ignored me before. Boys *always* stopped when I told them to. They had *always* begrudgingly respected my wishes and stopped.

My head began to pound and my body was hot. I was feeling sick.

"Theresa, please. I want you so badly."

I didn't want to do this. I was waiting until I was married to give my virginity. And I had already promised it to one certain man.

"Daniel, I'm a virgin. Please stop now!"

My head was spinning. I was terrified. With my hands against his chest, I pushed with all my strength, trying to shove his body off mine. I felt like I was suffocating. The more I struggled, the heavier he became. The room spun. I was pinned down like a butterfly on a board, unable to move my arms or legs. Pain throbbed in my head. Jim would be angry if I didn't stop this.

"Daniel," I begged. "Please stop! Get off..."

And then I felt it. Like a thousand knives shooting through me, ripping my insides to pieces. Pain like fire. I cried out.

Daniel pushed himself up and looked me in the eyes. "Theresa, you were telling the truth?"

I looked down between my legs and stared at the blood soaked sheets. My track shorts around my knees.

Speechless and in shock, I felt sick.

"Wait here," Daniel said.

Moments later I heard water running in the distance. Voices speaking foreign words came from other rooms. I yearned to run away and hide in the comfort of my own warm bed. But I was stuck in a house with no way of getting home. How could I go home, walk in the front door, face my mother, talk to Jim on our nightly phone call?

Overwhelmed with shame, I chastised myself for being naïve. For betraying myself. For betraying Jim, my parents, and God. Naked and bloody, my head pounding, I blacked out.

I felt Daniel shaking me.

"Theresa." He shook me again. "Theresa."

Reluctantly I opened my eyes.

"Come here with me, Theresa." Daniel was back. "Be quiet."

His hand on my elbow, I followed obediently.

"I didn't know," he said. "I thought you were just saying that."

He led me to the bathroom and closed the door. He motioned

towards the tub and I stepped in. Sinking into the water, new pain stabbed my privates, jolting me to reality. I was in a stranger's home. People I didn't know were milling around downstairs. People who probably didn't know I was here. I was laying naked, in front of a young man, feeling as if I was bleeding to death.

And I had lost something vitally important. My virginity.

Tears streamed down my face. How would I get home and what would I say to my mother and my boyfriend?

Outside the bathroom door I heard Daniel's voice. His voice rose and a new wave of fear washed over me.

"No! Leave her alone," he repeated.

I shivered. Had someone discovered I was here? I scrambled out of the tub, and doubled over in pain.

"You will not," I heard Daniel say. "She had nothing to do with this."

What was he talking about? Gingerly, I slipped into my clothes that Daniel had brought in. *For having just raped me, he sure was being considerate.*

Daniel snuck me out of the now bustling house and into his car. We were silent while he drove me home. I don't know how he knew where I lived. I never told him my address. Unable to look at Daniel, I got out of the car, entered the house, and went straight upstairs to the bathroom. I stripped off my soiled track uniform and threw it in the dirty laundry basket. My head in a fog, I ran a steaming hot bath.

"T? Is that you?" My mom knocked on the bathroom door. "Are you OK?"

"Yeah, mom," I said, unwilling and unable to tell the truth about what had just happened. "Had a rough practice and started my period. I'm taking a bath and going to bed."

Alone in the tub, I grieved what I was sure would be the worst thing that happened in my life. But that awful afternoon failed to compare with what was to come.

10.

Manipulation

Pleading sore muscles from track and menstrual cramps, I evaded school for several days. Depression swooped over me like a shadow and I felt separated from my body. I didn't leave my room, didn't accept Jim's phone calls, and couldn't write the daily letters we had exchanged for the past year.

How could I act as if nothing happened? Guilt was suffocating. Then the voices started. *It had been my fault. I could have prevented it. I should have done something. I shouldn't have gone with him.* I berated myself with the same accusations I would later hear from others.

Daniel called my private line several times but I ignored the phone. The deep, suave, slightly accented voice that once made my knees wobble now churned my stomach.

When I could no longer escape school, I returned. I got through the day without seeing Daniel. I didn't go to the school store and he never stayed for lunch. Instead, he went out with his Chaldean friends, or returned home for a hot cooked meal provided by his mother, aunts, or grandmother.

That afternoon, I turned the corner of the hall to go to my locker and stopped dead in my tracks. Leaning against my locker, arms crossed over his chest, Daniel was waiting for me.

"Why haven't you answered my calls? I need to talk to you," he whispered. "It's urgent."

I stared at him.

"I'm sorry," he said.

I wanted to believe his apology. But the part of me I had been saving for marriage, was gone. He had stolen it.

"I'm sorry you didn't listen to me," I replied. "You should have believed me. You've ruined everything. I have a boyfriend."

I wanted him to feel bad. Did he want me to tell him that it was OK? That I understood he hadn't respected me or listened to my wants or needs? In one act, he had ruined my life.

"We need to talk," he urged. "Really. There is a problem. I'm sorry." He was talking too fast. Mechanically. As if it was a well practice speech. "Skip track practice and meet me at my car. It is a matter of life or death."

I was tired of hearing him apologize. I didn't believe it for a second. Nor did it matter anymore. The bell rang and I turned and ran to class. In study hall, I sat next to the only other people who might know something; the two Chaldean misfit cousins. No longer bubbly, I was somber and sullen.

I gave the least amount of information as possible. On their advice, I decided to meet Daniel. I justified that my Catholic religion teachings mandated that I forgive. What Daniel had done was between him and God. I would have to battle with it every day, but so would he.

In the parking lot, next to his fancy, expensive car, Daniel held a white envelope. "I almost wish you hadn't come," he said.

"You said it was a life or death situation. Whose?"

"Yours."

Fear swept over me.

He continued, "Something terrible happened. The day we were together. I really am sorry about that. If I could take it back, I would."

"Well, you can't."

"I thought we were the only ones in the house that day, but we weren't. My cousins come to my house after school. They must have come in after we had been in my room for a while. I am really sorry."

I couldn't figure it out. If they had come in later, then they had witnessed him raping me. Why was my life in jeopardy?

"Theresa, I don't know how to tell you this, but they saw us together. They took pictures of you."

Bile rose into my throat. My knees buckled and I reached for the hood of his car for support. Daniel reached to help me.

I recoiled. "Don't touch me!"

"They told me they will give the photos to your dad if you don't do things for them. You have to earn the pictures or they will hang them around the school, church, and show your friends. They are cruel. You must do what they say."

I remembered the time they had threatened me at school.

"I tried talking them out of it," Daniel continued. "But they want you. You have to work for them to get the pictures back."

"What do you mean, Daniel? I don't believe you. Nobody would do that. Why? What do I have to do to earn them back? I don't understand. Like work in your family's store or something? Like do their homework?"

Daniel stood there for a long time. He slowly reached into the envelope and pulled out a picture. He looked at the image, and sadly handed it to me.

The photo showed my arms on his shoulders, partially clothed bodies intertwined, appearing to be not rape, but looking like a romantic, sexual union. Tears rolled down my cheeks. How would my father view this? What would it do to his career if they showed them to his boss? What would Jimmy think if he saw it? The priest at church, the youth group I sang in, my brothers, teachers, and my friends who knew I had a crush on Daniel. They would believe what they saw. They wouldn't believe my explanation. I had no proof that it had actually been rape.

His cousins knew this. Daniel knew it, too. I looked up at him. "Now what?"

"They want you to meet them tonight at my house to earn the pictures. You have to have sex with them. Do whatever they say and then they will give you the pictures. They promised me. I even talked to my older brother, Jonathan. They listen to him but he said he won't do anything. I tried Theresa. I'm sorry. It's all my fault. I told them what really happened and they didn't believe me. I told them you don't do this. Your not that kind of girl. But they don't care. Theresa, if you don't do this, they will hurt your brothers. They know a lot about you and your family. They know where your dad works and that he is gone a lot. And you and your brother walk to school."

I was too stunned to talk.

"They have things they can do to people. Theresa, just do what they say and it will be over soon. Then you can go your own way and no one will ever know anything. Please. I will keep trying to talk to them. I will try to help."

"You've done enough already, Daniel. I just can't do that. I'm not that kind of girl. You know that. I have to think about this. About what I'm going to do."

"Don't take too long. They are serious, Theresa. I've seen what they have done to others who didn't do what they wanted. I don't want that to happen to you," he said. "I like you a lot."

I turned to walk home, yearning to go somewhere safe where I could hide. I saw my brother, Allen, walking home. I could tell he was upset. Since our move to this place, he had seen me upset plenty of times, too. This house, this town, there was something terribly wrong here. Allen and I got along one minute, laughing on our way home from school and then, the moment we entered the house, it felt like a black cloud dropped over us and destroyed the mood. We joked that we lived in a $300,000 haunted house. We tried to make the best of it, waiting to move again in a few years.

It took a toll on our family. At school Allen was teased. Sensitive and emotional, he couldn't defend himself well. At home, my brothers and I fought constantly, even my parents fought when my dad was home from his many business trips. Mom questioned his late nights with customers at local bars. Depressed, she shut herself away in her bedroom, leaving me to care for the home and my brothers.

My mind raced as we walked home from school. I didn't want to shame my family, to add to their burden. The tension at home was building. Ironically, my parents accused Jimmy and me of being sexually active, even though we weren't.

Surely these men wouldn't make me do anything really bad. They were bluffing.

Allen slowed. "Hey T," he said. "There's a car following us. I'm scared."

An expensive, black car with tinted windows followed at a distance. They were letting me know they were there.

"It's OK, Allen," I said. "Let's cut through the neighbor's yard. I'll race you."

II

Cultural Rules

Once I got my drivers license, my parents purchased an old Ford Torino I named Dino after the dinosaur. Far from pretty, the brown, two door with burgundy leather interior was my key to freedom.

To pay for my freedom, I took a part-time job at the Burger King at the end of the street. The kids who worked there hung out together after work. During the day, Birmingham was an upper-middle class neighborhood with large homes, flower lined streets, and grassy parks. When the sun went down, the same streets were transformed into a dangerous place.

One night, I went out with a Jewish girlfriend. I drove to the Burger King to say hello to my co-workers and see if there were any leftovers. Pulling into the parking lot, I saw a commotion in the drive. Two groups of kids faced each other. Fists raised, they screamed profanities at one another. They swung sticks connected by a chain.

"Those are num-chucks," my friend explained. "The guys use them for fighting. Especially the Arabic boys."

Suddenly the boys flung the weapons at each other. Everyone was running, falling to the ground, and bleeding. I turned the car and sped away.

"It's a turf fight."

"You mean like in those 1950's movies?"

"It was Arab boys fighting Jewish boys. Other towns are strictly divided and only one or two types live there. But here, because of the money, many different rich kids all live in the same neighborhood and go to the same school. At night, they fight for the power."

The sight of their spilt blood stayed with me. I told my parents what I had seen, and my mom compared it to Northern Ireland. People fighting for something that had started many years ago and continued because it was a way of life. My dad set new rules that included me staying closer to home after dark.

I could tell that power and control set the tone for the entire city, no matter what part someone visited. People knew who had the power by what kind of convenience, grocery, or liquor stores were in the area and whose last name was on the signs. Another indicator was the types of churches, mosques, or temples in the area.

Within our church, there was a mixture of Chaldeans and others. We attended the same school, yet were divided when we congregated at the church. We sat on different sides and did not mingle, not even for fundraisers or festivals. I wondered if we really even shared a common bond of religion.

I sang in the church youth choir. It was all white kids and one Chaldean girl my age who sang like an angel. She did not talk much or socialize in the youth group, attend the popular retreat weekends or other activities. Just practice and singing on Sundays. One day, I went over to Nicole's house to practice a particularly difficult song for Christmas and her mother wouldn't speak to me. All the women in the house ignored me and Nicole barely tolerated me being in her home. I attempted to start conversation, initiate small talk by inquiring about her culture and commenting on her lovely home, but there was no response. The message was clear; I was not welcome there. The two of us couldn't mix, couldn't be friends.

12.

Terms of Indebtedness

The harsh jangle of the phone jarred me from sleep and I clumsily reached for the phone near my bed. "Theresa, I need to see you right now. It's urgent." I recognized the voice. It was Daniel. The icy fingers of fear gripped my heart.

"Are you crazy? My parents are here. I'll get in trouble. I'm not allowed out this late – "

He didn't let me finish. "This isn't an option. This is it. They want to meet with you right now."

"When?"

"I'll pick you up right away."

"Where?"

"Behind your house. On the street before yours."

"Why?"

"I mean it. You have to do this or they'll tell your dad. They are prepared to hurt you if you don't come. I'll meet you in ten minutes."

Within a half hour, I was back in the foreign home. The memory of my blood floating in their bathtub came rushing back. Daniel snuck me in through the back door and down the stairs. The steep, richly-carpeted stairs led to a door. He opened the door to an elaborately decorated basement. The large living room smelled of musk and other foreign scents I couldn't identify. A big screen TV, huge stereo system, and oversized furniture gave the room a masculine feel.

After my eyes adjusted to the dim light, I saw six men sitting, smoking, drinking coffee and talking in Arabic. Dressed impeccably, I guessed they were in their twenties. I grew more nervous by the second. They appeared to laugh at me, amused by my presence. Unsure of what to do, I looked at Daniel.

As if on cue, his two cousins came around the corner and into the main room. The same two who spit in my face at my locker. A fresh wave of fear washed over me and I grabbed Daniel's arm, chiding myself for turning to the person who started all this mayhem.

"Well, nice to have you here, Theresa."

Yeah, right, nice for you.

"As Daniel told you, we have something you want. But there is a condition. You will have to earn them back. And if you don't, not as if you have a choice," he paused, looking at his companion and laughing as he spoke, "there will be consequences. Are you prepared to do that?"

I stared at him. *What was I supposed to say?*

"Follow me," the other cousin demanded.

I looked at Daniel. "Come on, guys," he pleaded. "Do you really have to do this? It isn't her fault, come on!"

The short and stocky cousin, Nick, looked at me. "Do you want the photos or not?"

Daniel and I exchanged looks. He just shrugged. I hung my head and followed his cousin, still not understanding what would be demanded of me. We walked through the large room to an area that opened to two other rooms. Bedrooms, I guessed. One of the doors was closed.

Nick led me to the open door. In the large bedroom, gold and burgundy silk fabrics covered a four poster mahogany bed. It was the largest bed I had ever seen. No matter how financially well off my parents were, I had never seen money like this. Mirrors were on the walls and the ceiling. This place and the people in it reeked of money, masculinity, and power.

Behind me the door slammed. Daniel's quieter cousin had followed and locked the door, locking Daniel outside. I was instantly terrified. Why did I want him here, wishing he was protecting me? It made no sense. He was the one who broke my heart and brought me to this scary situation.

"You will do as I say," Nick ordered. "Whatever I say. You want the pictures back? You want to keep your family safe? You want your Daddy not to find out that you aren't his little princess anymore? To know you did the dirty little deed? That you're no longer a virgin?"

I thought I would choke on the lump that formed in my throat as he listed my sins.

He leaned close, his breath hot on my face. "You want to keep your sweet little puppy alive? Keep your brothers safe? Make sure nothing happens to your mother and father?"

I meekly nodded.

"Don't even think about telling anyone, or not obeying. I will personally deliver the photos to your father at work. Show his boss. Our priest at church. The kids you sing with. Post them at school for everyone to see."

The memory of him spitting in my face while the campus police pretended not to see assured me he was not bluffing.

"All right, you work for me. Work off the pictures." He fingered my hair and I cringed. "With that creamy, white skin and blonde hair, you will be an asset to my business." He let my hair drop back into place. "When you have done as I say, I will give you the pictures. And only then."

I thought of the humiliation I would feel if the priest and kids at school saw those damning photos. My dog I raised from a puppy, chosen from a box at the farmer's market in southern Indiana. Mostly, I didn't want my father to learn that I was no longer a virgin. I wanted to protect my mother and brothers while my dad was away traveling. To allow him to keep working there and keep our reputation safe.

I don't remember how I ended up on the bed, but I remember Nick's weight pressing upon me, telling me to be quiet, forcing himself into me. Not only did I endure excruciating pain, but I was shocked at the brutality of the act. Before I could begin to recover from the assault, the quiet cousin was on me, taking advantage of me for his own selfish pleasure. Tears ran down my face.

The ruthless pounding against my tender flesh caused my vision to go dark. I was nearing unconsciousness when the torture stopped. I waited a few minutes, afraid to open my eyes and find another man waited his turn. Unable to take another, I cautiously opened my eyes.

I was alone, naked and struggling to keep from vomiting due to the smell of a mixture of body fluids. Again, tears coursed down my cheeks.

The door opened and I cowered. It was Daniel. Entering slowly, he looked at me with pity. He started to say, 'I'm sorry,' but I cut him off.

"Shut up, Daniel," I hissed. "This is all your fault."

Scrambling about, I found my clothes and dressed. Within an hour, I was back home, transported in silence by Daniel. In my room, I ran the bath, not caring if anyone heard. I soaked in the tub without interruption. My family slept soundly. Soaking my bruised body, I relived over and over again the horror that I had experienced. Trying to soak away the sins of the night, the evil that had victimized my body. As I reached for a clean towel to dry off, I realized I had walked away without the pictures.

13.

The Horror Returns

After long days at school and afternoons of homework, I dropped exhausted into bed. Around midnight the phone would ring. Not bothering to brush my hair, or apply make-up, or change into clothes. Barefoot, I tiptoed down the long hallway past my parent's closed bedroom door. Slowly turning the corner, step by step I made my way to the main floor without waking anyone. I moved quietly through the entry hallway, past the den, and through the family room toward the sliding glass doors that led to the backyard. Silently, I unlocked the door, slid it open one inch at a time until I could squeeze my body through. Closing the door, I left it slightly open for my return.

Outside, I ran through the heavily landscaped backyard, the water fountain statue, and to the neighbor's yard. Rounding the front of their house, I arrived at the side street of our suburb. The car was always the same. The driver was always the same. Then came the torture and abuse.

This was the routine several nights a week. The only thing that changed was where I was. I never knew where I was being driven to, what the address was, or even what part of town I was in. Usually the location was a remote section of a large, impressive home. Each time, men I didn't know locked me away in a room for hours. I never knew the names of the blurry faces or the naked bodies that mounted me over and over again. Men of all ages. Men with money and always of Arabic decent.

No one asked why I was there, how old I was, who I was, or if they could help me. Nor was I a participant in the act. I didn't pretend that I enjoyed. I didn't dress up in lingerie. Or beg for their attention so I could service them.

I was a slave. Enslaved to serve whoever had been granted permission to walk through the locked bedroom door. Where I lay waiting. In bondage, trying to earn something. To them I was the end of a business deal.

The men in charge made sure I couldn't get away. If I escaped their hold, I had no way home. I didn't even know where I was. Nick's threats still rang in my ears. I couldn't leave until they were finished with me.

One night, an Arabic mother was angry at being locked out of the basement living area. These finished areas looked like they were designed as sacred dens for men only. Perhaps she heard my screams. Did she know what they were doing? The torture and agony I experienced so often by so many?

The woman pounded on the locked basement door while I was there with numerous men. She was furious.

"Nick, open this door," she demanded. "I will tell your mother. I am tired of this. Daniel, come up here right this minute. I won't permit this any longer. I am going to tell your father."

The men snickered. Through the locked door, they tried to convince her she had misunderstood and told her to go away. Her fury and yelling didn't phase them but I was scared. What would happen if she found me there? Would she call my parents?

She pounded on the door. "I'll go find the keys."

Nick turned to Daniel. "Get her out of here, now!"

"How? We can't take her up the stairs and out that door."

Nick looked at the small window at the top of the basement wall. I followed his gaze. It was one of those ugly, small windows with the plastic cone outside to keep away leaves. Like most of those windows, it was half full of grass, leaves, and cobwebs. I was afraid to think of what bugs or little animals living there, too. The window was about two feet by three feet. *How would I fit through that little window?*

A chair was dragged over and Daniel opened the window. He helped me onto the chair, grabbed my legs and pushed me through the small opening.

"Run quietly around the side of the house, to my car. I'll meet you there when I can," he explained.

Squeezing out like toothpaste from a tube, ignoring what I was touching or what was touching me, I heard the woman pounding on the door and yelling in her strong accent. The regular threats against my family, the continuous exploitation, and sleep deprivation acted as a brainwashing. I was convinced that being discovered by this woman would be worse than what I was experiencing. Only later did it occur to me that she might have been my way out. Being found may have been the vehicle I needed to stop the torture.

When I reached Daniel's Trans Am, I crouched down low on the gravel driveway near the passenger door, waiting for him. After what seemed like an eternity, he came and took me home.

****

That spring, it was impossible to enjoy my favorite season. Though I tried to work hard enough for the photos, it was never enough.

"Next time." The disappointing answer was always the same. "Next time."

I was strained to the breaking point trying to maintain friends who knew nothing of my dark secret, keeping a smile on my face at home, running on the track team, and keeping my private horror from my long distance boyfriend.

In May my mom and I prepared to travel to Cleveland for my first formal dance. Jim and I went to dinner with his friends and went to the prom. The boys were focused on partying, drinking, and getting to the hotel rooms they had successfully rented. Jimmy and I had our turn in the room, but remained true to the vow we shared. Jimmy let his friends believe we were like all the other teens and didn't elude to the fact that we hadn't had sex. Many times that night I wanted to share my torture with him. To ask him to save me. To take away the pain. To make the nightmare stop.

But I was afraid for him. If he knew what was happening, he could be hurt. I was afraid I would lose him if he found out I was a long way from being a virgin. I was more frightened of the consequences of revealing the secret than continuing to live it. I kept my mouth shut.

But I wondered, *Was it happening to other girls, too? Was there more to it than lustful, cruel, evil men? Was I a pawn in a far larger, danger-*

ous game? Those nights when I was raped by Chaldean men, I had over-heard things I didn't understand. On an international level, the United States wasn't happy with the Middle Eastern countries. Prices for oil and gasoline were rising. Inflation was rampant. War seemed eminent. I could feel the tension, even in Detroit.

I had heard that many Arabic boys and men traveled back to the Middle East to get re-acquainted with family members during the summer. They took money and brought people back into our country. Those who remained stateside, worked full time in their father's stores. Regardless of the reason for the reprieve, I was grateful for the chance to recover and attempt to heal my soul and body.

A modeling agency approached me that summer and invited me to take modeling classes. It was nice to feel beautiful again. My mom went with me to meet with the director of the agency.

"What do you want with my daughter?"

I shrunk in the chair, wishing she would be nice and not ruin this chance for me to do something positive with my looks.

"Your daughter has a unique beauty. She holds a great deal of expression in her face and has a beautiful smile. With the right training she could make a lot of money. Money for college."

"What kind of training?"

"First, we need photos. She'll have a make over with a professional makeup artist, her hair done, and you could take pictures on your own to save money. Just to see if she looks good for the camera."

"And after that?"

"It's one hundred dollars for the hair and make up. If the pictures are good, then she would be signed on for jobs. She needs classes to learn how to move, which would be recouped with the money she makes."

Mom narrowed her eyes. Though my parents were financially well-off, things like this were not a priority. Clothing and material items were not of value to them. Family and vacations and nice houses were more important. She looked around the room. Not at the glamorous pictures of women on the walls, but at the couch in his office. "We'll think about it."

The following week, I had my makeover and hair done. Jimmy was coming to see me with some of his guy friends so I scheduled it the day of his arrival. The makeover took hours, sitting still while I was painted, my hair rolled and teased and sprayed. At the end of what seemed like forever, I looked in the mirror. I was beautiful.

My mom located several used gowns from friends and the local Goodwill store. Dad proudly took the pictures. My favorite was a gold lame´ turtleneck, long sleeve gown that matched the natural gold in my hair. I looked like a slender, sleek model.

Jim arrived that night to see a new me. I was proud of how I looked. After hours of preparation, his response crushed me. "I liked you the way you were," he said.

I ran to the bathroom and removed pounds of paint. I felt rejected, disappointed that he wasn't happy for me. He couldn't accept that I was growing up; he would never accept the secret I had carried the last few months. I would never be able to tell him what was happening. Though he said he loved me, it was conditional. My captors had taken Jim away from me, too.

We submitted the pictures to the agency and they called to meet with my mother again. I stood close, listening in as she spoke on the phone. "Mmm, hmm," she murmured. "Yes."

I was hopeful. Without anything good left in my life, I wanted this badly. I needed it. For my sanity.

"I don't think we're interested. We move a lot and she couldn't commit to doing it for long term. Considering the amount of money involved, I don't think it would be advisable," she concluded.

I looked at my mom in astonishment. "Why can't I? The pictures were great."

"It costs a lot of money," she explained. "We'll probably only be here for another year. This is a long-term thing. Besides, guys like that director only want young girls for one thing. You saw that couch in his office. He just wants our money and to have sex with you."

"But, mom – "

"And to be honest, you're vain enough already. I don't want you to get worse. Always primping in front of the mirror. It's for your own good," she said flatly. "End of conversation."

The couch was the last thing I was worried about. I had been enduring endless nights of torture that she didn't know about, and she was worried that this man would want to have sex with me? *How comical. How ironic. My chance to have a normal life cut short because she thought a man would want to have sex with me.*

I began to look for a way out. I needed a protector. Someone older to help me escape. I went to the private community pool daily with my friends. My body was budding into a woman and I sensed that I had a sort of power over men. Older boys and men sensed my developing sexuality. I liked using the new power to gain control over men, instead of them controlling me.

I showed interest in two guys that were four years older. When we were alone, I told them what was happening and that I needed their help.

"You're one of the Chaldean's girls?" one asked. That was the last time they spoke to me.

I bonded with a nice young man from work. He was several years older than me, a bit of a nerd, a good athlete, hadn't gone to college and never had a girlfriend. He had big, fuzzy hair, large glasses, and was aspiring to be a manager at Burger King, though he wished he had pursued his dream of playing professional baseball. I hoped he would protect me. I believe he was looking for his first sexual experience. If the Arabs saw I had a boyfriend, perhaps they would leave me alone when school began. Yet he ran fast from the danger, abandoning me to endure my ongoing nightmare. I paid an even higher price when the Chaldeans realized what I had attempted to do.

I was in this alone. It was my nightmare. My torture to endure until I either died or got away. And only 16 years old.

14

Calm before the Storm

School started before I was ready. Summer had been a taste of normal with sleep filled nights, shifts at the fast food job, and vacation with my family.

We took our pop-up camper, loaded the van, and spent the days sightseeing in Toronto and our nights telling ghost stories around the campfire with my cousins. It was a healing time.

When school resumed, so did my life as a sex slave. Once again I was the mouse caught by the cat. A good hard swat from the cat stunned the mouse into temporary unconsciousness. Dazed, the mouse attempted to run away. The cat pounced again. Over and over. Until the mouse resigned itself to the game and a long tortuous death.

On the first day of my junior year in high school, I proceeded from class to class. Happy from the restful summer, I was apprehensive about my fate. My grades had fallen at the end of my sophomore year as a result of the physical and emotional trauma I silently endured. Lack of sleep made it difficult to concentrate. It was crucial I buckle down and raise my grades for college.

After lunch, I went to Business Math. Math wasn't my strong suit and I was in the remedial class. I entered the classroom and selected a seat at one of the eight-foot tables. Pretending to read was how I entered a new situation. I kept my head down until I made friends.

Without looking up, I felt him enter the room. Chills went down my spine. Daniel took a seat at the table directly in front of me and arrogantly leaned back in his chair, inches from me.

When I thought it couldn't get worse, his cousins entered the classroom. Their entrance was loud, letting everyone know they were important. Geeky and mouse-like, the instructor became nervous when he saw them. My face was hot, the heat rising up my neck and into my cheeks.

Nick and his sidekick whooped and hollered when they saw me. Their comments were in Arabic as they elbowed each other in the ribs and smiled smugly. Like Samantha in the 70's TV show *Bewitched*, I wanted to twitch my nose and instantly be anywhere but there. Anywhere. How would I survive this? I needed help if I wanted to survive another year.

Jim graduated high school the summer before. We hadn't seen each other because he worked full time and I had been away on vacation. He said he would visit for a few days. I thought this might be the perfect timing for my protector to take over. To take a stance at the beginning of the school year. If I could show the Chaldeans that I had someone to protect me, maybe they would back off. I hoped and prayed that I wouldn't have to endure this horror for another year.

Jim borrowed a buddy's car and drove the two hours from Cleveland to Birmingham. We spent a great weekend at my house and went sight seeing in Detroit. My mom took us to Greek town and we walked around the big city, playing on the river front. He planned to come to school with me on Monday and leave that evening to get back in time for work.

I didn't have the courage or heart to tell him what was happening to me. It was a double-edged sword. On one hand, he would be disappointed, crushed, and might break up with me if he found out. Or, his Italian anger would surface and he would fight them and possibly get hurt. These guys were ruthless. Not only had they back-handed me across the mouth numerous times, but I'd seen them in street fights, blood gushing everywhere. I desperately wanted out, but not at the expense of my future husband.

Jim didn't make it through the entire day at my school. He sat next to me in my classes, and walked with me to my locker. With Jim by my side, I gave the evil cousins a smug look as I passed them in the hall. Jim was handsome and deeply muscled.

During science class, Jim said he needed to go to the bathroom. He got a pass from the teacher and I told him where to find it. He was gone a long time and when he returned, he was different. Quiet. Not his usual smiling, fun-natured self.

"I'm going back to the house," he said after the bell rang.

"Are you feeling OK?"

"Fine."

"But –"

He bolted through the school doors, abandoning me to face the Chaldeans during math class, alone.

At lunch, my friends asked where Jim was. I told everyone that he had gotten suddenly sick. I left the lunchroom to walk down the hall, trying not to make eye contact with Nick. As we passed, he gave me a snide look and said something in Arabic. I wondered if he had something to do with Jim's quick exit.

It didn't matter. The rest of the day, I felt more alone than ever before. I had been hopeful that it was finally over. I thought Jim would be my protector and save me from further abuse. That I wouldn't have to tell him what was happening to me. That the Chaldeans would see him and leave me alone.

I was naïve, unaware of how much I was benefiting someone else's business through my body and my pain. They would not let me simply walk away. They were making too much money off me.

After school, I found that Jim was gone. He went back home. No note, no explanation, no good-bye. *What did he know? What had he heard? Were we finished? Had I lost him, too?*

Jim and I never spoke of that day, even years later. It took twenty years for him to ask what had happened to me back then. But I knew, even then, that it would kill him to hear the truth. That he wouldn't be able to handle it. Nor did I have the courage to ask him what had happened to him in the bathroom. We brushed it under the rug, silently agreeing to never discuss it. Nor did I tell him of the price I paid for leaning on him to be my protector. I never tried to find a protector again.

15.
Submitting

A car honked as I walked home from school. My brother, Allen stayed after school for a Christian group meeting. I walked along the sidewalk next to the busy 13 Mile Road. Occasionally, a car horn honked or a man whistled. I hated the attention. Unlike the rural areas where I had grown up, in this upbeat city, men frequently honked at girls. When I complained about it to my mom, she viewed the acknowledgement as a compliment. She told me to wave back and say thanks.

But I didn't want to acknowledge it. The less attention I brought to myself, the better. I certainly didn't need anymore of that. The physical and sexual attraction was not wanted. Every time I heard a car horn, I wanted to hide under a rock.

On this day, I sensed a car following me for about a half mile. Being continuously on guard was exhausting. Cars parked outside my home, stopped by my work where the cousins stood silent in the doorway. Watching. Reminding me that I couldn't escape and I better keep quiet. Living in my own home during the slavery, I was still a prisoner.

The expensive car stopped beside me and the driver's tinted window rolled down. The Chaldean's face was vaguely familiar. Early twenties, not handsome, dressed in expensive clothes and embellished with plenty of gold jewelry.

A flashback jolted through me. He was one of the many men who had forced himself on me. He had been exceptionally brutal. I began to tremble.

"Get in," he demanded.

"Where's Daniel? I didn't hear I was supposed to go anywhere," I stammered.

"Get in now." He pointed to the seat next to him. A large, sharp knife lay on the passenger seat.

I looked at him, then at the knife, and then straight ahead. My house was only a half-mile away. *Was anyone watching? Would anyone see me get in his car? Could I take a chance and risk running home?*

He picked up the knife and pointed it at me. Imagining the sharpness of the blade across my skin, I opened the door and sat down in the passenger seat. It felt all wrong. It wasn't like all the other times.

As we drove off, he rested the knife on my leg. I wanted to open the car door and jump out, but sat frozen. Like cold water in my face, I realized I could handle any sex act, but I was afraid of being stabbed.

He drove me to a remote area, and pulled the car into a vacant parking lot. Then his hands were on me, tearing at my clothes.

I fought him. Suddenly the knife was at my throat.

"I'm tired of sharing you, waiting my turn, earning my time," he growled. Cruel, he forced my body to his will.

"I wanted you all for myself," he said afterwards.

The knife lay between us as he drove me back to my subdivision. He opened the door for me to get out. Broken in spirit, feeling alone and helpless, I got home just as Allen walked through the door. It looked natural to my mother for the two of us to come home at the same time. I climbed the stairs and headed straight to the bathroom where I ran the water and soaked in a long, hot bath.

Thankfully the cousins were not in math class the following day. They rarely came anyway. On the days they did appear, there was a marked difference in the way the teacher taught. A timid and reserved man, he ignored the callous remarks by the cousins in their native language.

With thoughts of the day before and Daniel sitting inches from me, all I saw were jumbled numbers on the board. A tightly-folded piece of paper landed in front of me on my open book. I slowly unfolded the paper.

The chicken scratch read, "They want to see you tonight."

That night I arrived, plagued with memories of the rape by the unknown Chaldean man the day before. I knew they would find out. They knew everything that happened in my life. Would there be repercussions? Would I have to pay another price for this decision? I was scared.

In the living area of the home I was accustomed to being taken to, Nick approached me. He rarely spoke to me and I shrunk back in fear.

"I have a question. It is important that you answer correctly. For your own good. Do you understand?"

I nodded, a lump in my throat.

"Were you with another Chaldean this week?"

Should I lie? Will I get out of here alive? "Yes. He told me you said it was OK. I thought he was taking me to you. Afterwards, he said he lied and wanted me all for himself."

Nick turned and left the room. I was terrified that I was going to be punished. The others in the room went about their business, soon forgetting I was there. I overheard his voice in the other room, barking orders and yelling. I don't know what happened but I didn't have to have sex with any men that day. I didn't see the unknown man again for a very long time.

16.
Proposal

One morning, my mom told me she had a meeting for the international exchange program where she had recently started working. She was excited; glad to have something to do that was constructive, creative, and helpful to others. Her schedule included meetings several days each week, play practice in the evenings, attending the Gourmet Club several times per month, and entertaining my dad's customers to help him close deals when he was in town. This schedule got her out of the house and kept her busy since dad was frequently away, traveling for work.

"Theresa, you're in charge of dinner tonight," she said that morning. Her busy calendar often resulted in additional responsibilities for me. "I won't get back until late and your dad won't be back until the end of the week."

School was uneventful that day. I hoped to get through the day without incident. I went to honors English, the only class I was successful at, then tried to focus on raising my falling grades in my other classes. It was difficult to concentrate, wondering what would happen next. When the phone would ring again. When a note would come, demanding my body this afternoon or in the night.

My last class of the day was study hall. Two of my Chaldean friends (the misfit cousins from speech class) sat with me. They tutored me in their language and I helped them write their speeches and English papers. Students noticed this. They saw me talk to the evil cousins and leave school in Daniel's car. The called me Chaldean Lover and Camel Jockey Lover. Even my girlfriends believed I liked Arab boys. Smiling and pretending on the outside, I cringed deep inside each time it was said or written in my high school yearbook.

I was writing an English paper for these misfit cousins when Bassim poked me in the arm.

"Hey, what ya' do that for man?"

"What man?"

"Look at the door."

There stood Daniel. *What was he doing here?* He was usually gone by now. Home or working at his family's store. Dread washed over me. Bassim and Hassam looked at me with sad eyes.

"Bye," they said, knowingly.

I gathered my books and gave the study hall monitor an excuse that I needed to get to track practice early. Silently, I followed Daniel to the car. He held open the door for me, though he was anything but a gentleman.

I never knew where we were going. Today we arrived at his house. The driveway was filled with cars. I shut my eyes against the growing feeling of doom.

Downstairs, Daniel led me to the bedroom. The second bedroom door was open. That was unusual because it was always closed. I tried to peek in to the man I'd heard so much about. Jonathan. He seemed to be the one in charge. Sometimes I'd heard him outside the room barking orders at the other men who either revered or feared him. Once I asked about him and was slapped across the face.

"Never mention him again," I was told as I rubbed my stinging cheek. "He doesn't exist. For your own good, don't ever say his name. Understood?"

Nick and the other cousin were waiting in the room for me. I shook at the sight of Nick, who had grown more ruthless in his treatment of me. Daniel had tried to step in a few times, telling him to stop, before I was hurt too badly.

"Strip and lay down," Nick ordered. "I have something special planned for you today."

I obeyed. Several other Arab men walked in the room as Nick shoved Daniel out the door. "You can't watch today," he told him.

"But – " Daniel began to protest.

"Out," Nick snapped.

Before the door closed, Daniel locked eyes with me and I saw his terror.

"You can't save her today, little cousin," Nick said and slammed and locked the door.

From a large dresser, Nick pulled several pieces of rope from the drawer. I'd had a bad feeling about the day and I nervously shivered. He spoke in Arabic to the other men. I understood a little, but not nearly enough. My Arabic lessons so far had only covered cuss words and names of food. But none of it helped in this situation. Was it better to know my fate ahead of time, or be oblivious of the eminent horror?

The other cousin grabbed my leg and jerked it to the far corner of the bed. I instinctively jerked my leg back and was instantly sorry for it. Nick twisted my ankle until I felt it would snap in two. I screamed in pain and someone began pounding on the door. Daniel.

Nick ignored the door and tied my ankle to the bed post. Then he tied my other leg to the opposite post. My twisted ankle swelled and my legs lost all sensation. I laid there spread eagle, humiliated at being crudely exposed. Tears of shame sprang to my eyes.

Smiling evilly, Nick grabbed my wrists. I whimpered and he laughed as he tied my arms to opposite bedposts. One by one, the men in the room mounted and abused me. They carried on conversation in their foreign language, oblivious to my pain and horror. I closed my eyes, but couldn't block out their voices, the smell of their bodies, the sound of their grunts and heavy breathing next to my ear.

How I longed to be untied, to return home to make dinner for my younger brothers. When the motion, the pounding, the jerking ended, I anticipated getting released. I opened my eyes to Nick's sinister grin, looming over me.

"We're not done yet, *Habbebe*."

I knew this word. It was Arabic for *sweetheart*. The last thing I felt like lying here like this.

"You thought that was it?"

Hope deflated at the sound of his words.

"I told you I have a special surprise for you. These men," he looked at the faces around me and they chuckled, "paid a dear price to be here today. You should feel honored."

Nick brought to the bed a collection of items and began abusing me physically with them as the men laughed.

I screamed in agony and pleaded with the men to stop. It only seemed to make Nick more determined to exacerbate my pain. In Arabic, he instructed one of the men to clamp his hand over my mouth as they continued abusing me. The large, heavy hand over my mouth muffled my screams and nearly suffocated me. From the pain, fear, and lack of air, I hyperventilated. From somewhere very far away, I heard pounding on the bedroom door.

The agony seemed to last for hours. Lack of circulation had caused my legs to go numb while the rest of my body burned with pain. I was in shock from the abuse. Mercifully, I lost consciousness.

When I awoke, I was naked on the bed, and cut free from the bondage. Seeing a man sitting next to me, I jumped. It was Daniel and he was holding my hand. I tried to move but was too bruised, the pain was too fierce.

Finally when I mustered enough strength to leave the bedroom, a deep, older voice boomed from down the hall. The outer room was suddenly quiet when they realized I was being summoned to him.

"Daniel, bring her in here." It was Jonathan.

I looked at Daniel and shook my head. I couldn't stand one more man having his way with me today.

"Now!" he boomed.

Ignoring my objection, Daniel took my hand and gently pushed me into the room. It was lavishly decorated with huge wooden furniture, expensive, richly colored materials. It resembled my idea of what a harem would look like, with luxurious, sheer hanging fabric. Before me, lounging comfortably upon his massive bed was a stunning Chaldean man in his late twenties. He slowly looked me over, approvingly.

"Leave Daniel," he said. "We won't be long."

With my eyes I begged Daniel not to leave, but he obeyed his older brother, turned and abandoned me once again.

"Theresa, do you know who I am?"

I was surprised that he knew my name. I also knew he was the one in charge. Behind the scenes, he was the one profiting from my exploitation.

"Jonathan?" I answered tentatively.

"I can make your life very easy or very hard. Do you know that?"

"How much harder can it be?" *Much worse and I would be dead.*

"I know. They treated you very hard today didn't they?"

I looked him in the eyes and nodded. Tears filled my eyes.

"I can take all that away. I can give you a very nice life. I can stop all the pain. Would you like that?"

I didn't know what to say.

"Let me put this simply. They will continue to hurt you and I will give them permission to do whatever they want to you. Or you can work for me. You have been a good addition to my cousin's business. Which in the long run benefits me as well. But I have decided that I want you to be my private charge. I will take care of you and protect you. But if you don't, I can't promise what will happen. Do you understand this?"

I nodded, though I did not know what he was talking about.

"Think about it. Don't talk to anyone about it. This is between us. Tell Daniel when you are ready to contact me."

As always, Daniel drove me home in silence. He stopped at the usual place behind my house. As I reached for the door handle, I looked back at him. "Did they give you the pictures?"

He looked down and slowly shook his head. No.

I snuck through the neighbor's yard and went into my house. After washing my face, I took the dinner out of the refrigerator that my mother had prepared earlier. Zombie-like, I put the dish in the oven.

"Allen," I called to my brother, "make a salad. I'll be upstairs until dinner is done cooking. Upstairs, my tears poured down my face as the bath water poured from the facet. Still crying uncontrollably, I climbed into the tub, every part of my body hurt, every organ was bruised. My soul was crushed.

17.
Watchful Eyes

It didn't take long to realize that I was at the Chaldean's mercy no matter where I was, what time it was, or what I was doing. I knew I was constantly watched but I had no idea to what extent.

I enjoyed babysitting and made spending money taking care of little kids. Being the oldest with three younger brothers, it came naturally. Getting away from home, eating cool snacks and pop that my mom would never buy was pleasant, but the best part was being out of the dreariness of our home, escaping my responsibilities, the fighting, and most importantly – the phone.

After the torturous afternoon with the cousins and the conversation with Jonathan, they mercifully left me alone for a few days. On the weekend I had a babysitting job for a family I'd not babysat for before. I liked that the fact that they lived in the country far from my suburban house. I felt safe as I put the kids to bed and settled down with a pop to watch a movie. We didn't have cable or movie channels at my house. I relaxed, thinking this was the easiest way anybody ever earned money.

When I heard the phone ring in the other room, I got up to answer it.

"Miller residence," I said.

"Theresa, what are you doing?"

I couldn't believe it. They were playing tricks on me. Perhaps I had fallen asleep in the chair and was having a nightmare. "How did you know where I was? How did you get this number?" *Oh my gosh, was he outside? I couldn't leave. I would be in so much trouble. I couldn't get out of this one. There were little kids here. I had to protect them.*

"We know where you are at all times, Theresa."

I began to shake. "What do you want? I can't leave here, no matter what!"

"Don't worry. They don't need you. Not right now, anyway. They just told me to call you and make sure you knew they are watching you. Be careful, Theresa. Jonathan is involved now. They know that and aren't going to want to lose you so easily. It changes everything."

"How did you get this number?"

I heard voices in the background and sounds like the phone had been yanked from Daniel's hands. The line went dead.

The Millers returned home an hour later. I was shaking as Mr. Miller drove me home.

"Are you all right?" he asked.

"I think I'm getting sick."

I watched to see if we were followed. At home, I checked in with my parents, telling them everything went well and that I was going to take a bath. Running the bath, I trembled to realize even my private time, my escapes were monitored. I could be located any time, anywhere. I was never safe. And my family was never safe either.

I wanted to disappear. Even my refuges weren't safe. They probably knew I was in the bathtub right at that moment. They knew when my father was out of town. They knew everything.

Tears of desperation flowed down my cheeks. How much would I have to endure? How much longer would I have to pay the price? What was the cost of getting the pictures back? Of keeping my family safe? Of staying alive?

18.
Remembering My Place

The stress of being constantly watched in addition to the brutal assaults on my body produced intense stress. Noticing my grades dropping and a difference in my personality, my parents arranged for counseling.

Week after week, I sat silent during the sessions. The woman talked about boys and typical stressors teens faced. She had no idea about the boys and stressors I dealt with on a daily basis. I rolled my eyes and stared out the office window. After a while, she resolved herself to my silence and gave me weekly lectures. Talking into the air, she discussed issues of self-esteem and valuing myself. Though I wouldn't admit it at the time, I listened. She made me yearn for good times to return to my life. I was weary of sneaking out at night, scared of getting caught, and more scared of the punishment I would receive if I didn't sneak out. I was exhausted from leading a double life, depleted from being tortured and used and over again.

After counseling one day, I was called at night. I felt stronger, determined to change my destiny. I wanted the pictures.

I never knew what the night would demand, and it was perpetually worse than I imagined. After he had been sexually satisfied, before I lost my nerve, I decided to ask. I stood in the room, naked, as he dressed. The other men were leaving the room, fully disregarding my presence.

"Nick, can I have the pictures now? I've done more than enough to earn them," I spoke shyly.

Not looking up, he remained silent.

"I think I have the right to them now," I pleaded.

All motion in the room stopped. The others stood in shocked silence. Nick slowly turned toward me. His facial expression reminded me that he was the most evil person.

"You have no rights here," he growled. "I own you and you will do as I say." He gripped the gold metal buckle of his belt and whipped it out of the loops. He laughed slowly, deeply, calculatingly. He swung the belt over his head and aimed it for my naked body. The snake-like belt made a hissing sound as it sailed through the air and struck my bare skin.

I screamed in pain and fell to my knees. He swung again, striking me across my back. From the corner of my eye, I saw Daniel lunge from the corner where he had been waiting.

"Don't even try it, Daniel," Nick warned. His eye on Daniel, he hit me a third time.

Turning to the others, he smiled and left the room.

I wept as I gingerly put on my clothes. I returned home, empty handed once more.

19.
Kidnapped

I was dangerously weary. Tired of the nightly abuse, too sleep deprived to keep up my grades in school, worried that the well being of my brothers, my mom, my dad's job – even my dog – would be hurt or ruined if I made a mistake. I was exhausted from hiding a hideous and growing secret from my family, classmates, and boyfriend.

I stopped writing letters to Jim. I stopped going to track practice. I sunk into a deep despair. My desire for life was gone.

I refused Jonathan's offer. I couldn't voluntarily do this. It was different now because I didn't have a choice. I was trying to keep my family safe until Nick gave me the photos. The shame of being found out, the risk of my father losing his job if they leaked the pictures to his boss, the responsibility of keeping my brothers out of harms way, all gave me no choice in the matter. I felt forced to finish this out until the end. Whatever that would be.

Jonathan's offer was to keep me as his prostitute. To work for him so he could offer me to wealthier, more powerful men. This wouldn't be small time guys like Nick; it would be a more dangerous game.

Daniel didn't like that I had told him no. He asked everyday if I was sure. Did I want to reconsider? My answer remained the same.

Instead of me helping Daniel with his math homework as I regularly did, he began asking me if I needed help with my homework. Even my Chaldean friends, Bassim and Haddam sensed the change in me. They noticed the dark circles under my eyes and my speech papers that passed by their desks with my failing grades. They realized all they had taught me would not be enough for my survival. There was a feeling of tension in the air, a brooding danger.

The weather grew colder as fall gave way to winter. The dreary weather matched my spirit. Mechanically I went through the motions. By the evening, I could no longer remember what I had done during the day. I wished, hoped, someone would care enough to intervene before

I ended up dead. Laying in bed that night, I sent out a prayer that the torture would soon be over. Numb to all feelings and emotions, I drifted off to sleep.

Hours later, I woke to the shrill sound of my personal phone. Sadly, I reached for the handle. I didn't need to hear the message. I didn't need to guess what or who it was. I knew.

"Theresa, I need to meet you. We really have to talk," Daniel said.

Groggily, I agreed. As if I had a choice.

"Things are about to change and you are in trouble. Can you meet me now?"

His words sent fresh fear coursing through my veins and I was instantly awake. I sensed that circumstances were about to get worse.

"What's wrong? What is happening? Daniel, I am scared."

"I know. I will explain in a little while."

"You have to help me," I pleaded.

"All I can tell you is that I talked to my older brother, Jonathan."

"I don't know how much longer I can do this."

He sighed. "Meet me in the usual place in ten minutes."

I believed that Jonathan was the leader of something even more sinister than what I was experiencing. My one mysterious encounter with him led me to wonder what was really going on. Was I earning pictures or was this only the surface? I had seen and heard hints of confidential business dealings that seemed to involve high stakes. The expensive houses, clothes, and jewelry in addition to the amounts of money I'd seen laying around proved that they weren't just working for their father's grocery stores. I suspected I was a pawn in a dangerous, mafia-type game. This was a life or death situation.

Though it was growing cold outside, I didn't risk the noise of pulling open my dresser drawers and changing clothes. My dad was home and I had to be extra careful not to wake my parents. I quietly opened my bedroom door, as I had done so many times before and crept past my parent's closed bedroom door. Sneaking down the stairs, I was careful not to make a single sound.

Barefooted, I tiptoed through my back yard. The cold dew soaked my feet as I snuck through the neighbor's yard, noticing the light on in their family room and the owner watching TV. I crouched behind the bushes so he wouldn't see me and quietly ran toward the street.

Under dim street lights, the neighborhood houses were quiet, the residents sound asleep. I never got used to waiting in this spot, waiting for the nightmare to begin all over again. Something felt odd tonight. My stomach churned nervously, fear induced adrenaline caused my heart to thunder in my ears.

I didn't have to wait long before the Trans-Am approached. Maybe tonight I would be released from bondage. Maybe they would give me the photos and leave me alone. As Daniel's car stopped in front of me, I felt the hairs on my arms stand straight up. I felt a tug on my shoulder, as if an angel was telling me not to go.

It was dark and I leaned in the passenger window. Arabic music played on the stereo. But Daniel wasn't in the driver seat.

"I thought Daniel was coming to talk to me," I said nervously.

"Yeah, we know," Nick replied. "We made him call you."

"Where is he? This is his car!"

"He won't be able to help you tonight. Get in."

I shrunk away from the car. Suddenly the car door opened and a strange Arabic man grabbed my waist and pulled me into the car. Fear surged though my veins and I struggled, trying to escape. I opened my mouth to scream, but a hand quickly shot out from somewhere, and struck me across the face. The blow made my head spin, and stars clouded my vision.

The door slammed shut and tires screeched as the driver sped from the subdivision. The inside of the car was filled with the cruel laughter of the men.

In shock, it took me a while to focus on where we were going and the surroundings. Outside the window, I saw we were in an unfamiliar, dark, poverty-riddled area of Detroit. The landscape was dotted with abandoned buildings, boarded up houses, and vacant lots. It smelled dirty.

If I escaped, where would I go? I had no idea where I was. Tears rolled down my cheeks. I understood a few words as the men talked a mixture of Arabic and English. Somehow I knew my survival was threatened tonight. Overwhelmed, I felt as if I was in another world. Far from the comforts of my bedroom in my nice home. None of that mattered at this moment.

Above the loud Arabic music, they spoke Arabic slang and laughed. The smell of their musky cologne mixed with the biting odor of alcohol that they passed around to each other. Someone pressed the bottle to my lips. I clenched my mouth tightly closed and was backhanded.

"Don't hurt her too much," I heard Nick caution from the front seat.

Gasping, I choked as hot liquid was dumped down my throat.

"We need her tonight," Nick continued. "Besides, he'll be mad if you hurt her."

The car slowed and pulled into a sleazy, dirty motel. Broken down cars parked in front of the doors to their rooms. I was half-carried, half-dragged into the hotel room. It smelled of old cigarette smoke. I saw a large, king-sized bed and dresser. There was a mirror, several chairs and a table. And two dozen Arabic men. More nasty tasting liquid was poured down my throat. It tasted different than the other liquid they had made me drink in the car. It was a familiar bitter flavor.

I was told to strip and lie on the bed. When I tried to keep my underpants on, the room erupted into laugher. They were torn from me, by unknown hands and I was shoved to the bed.

As I scanned the room, I saw the only two people I knew – the evil Chaldean cousins.

"The present has arrived for you all," Nick announced to the men. "For any that wish. His way of saying thank you for a job well done."

At some point during the night, I lost consciousness. I lost count of how many men took their turn and abused my body for their pleasure. The fact that I was there not of my own free will excited them. I blacked out from the intense trauma overload and the liquor laced with some drug. Who knows what happened to me after that point. Or for how long.

When I finally came too, my head was spinning and cloudy. I didn't want to open my eyes. I wanted to leave them closed for eternity. I listened. It was unusually quiet. Opening my eyes, I struggled to focus. The room was empty except for empty beer cans and liquor bottles strewn everywhere.

A wave of nausea caused me to bolt for the bathroom, but as I got to my feet, I doubled over as severe pain shot though my legs, my privates area, and my abdomen. I dropped to the floor, curled in the fetal position, gasping to breathe.

Eventually I got to my feet and wobbled to the toilet and violently threw up. After rinsing my mouth, I washed my face with cold water from the sink. I searched the room for my clothes, picked up the sheets, and looked under the bed. Standing there, vulnerable and naked, I felt the rise of bile once again in my throat. After I vomited the second time, I laid my head on the toilet seat in desperation. With my head facing the shower, I saw my clothes. They were in the bathtub, wet.

I put on my cold, wet pajama pants and t-shirt. My underwear were long gone, most likely carried off as someone's souvenir from the night's activities.

Part of me wanted to take a bath and soak my aching body. *Had I been left in the rundown motel because they thought I was dead? Were they trying to keep me captive? Knowing I had no way to return home. Forcing me to wait for them, for whatever future plans they had for me.*

I needed to escape fast before someone returned. Outside, the parking lot was dirty. Barefoot, wet, and cold, my head was still cloudy and my stomach churned. I didn't know where to go. I had no money, no identification, nothing. I didn't have anyone to call to come get me.

A small restaurant was at the rear of the motel. People were inside. *Maybe someone would give me a ride home. Maybe there was a way out of this situation after all. Maybe Daniel would show up, looking for me and take me back. What a nasty place. Who would eat here? What if someone knows those guys and they come back for me? Should I hide?*

Entering the lobby, I saw about six people sitting at booths, smoking, chatting, and eating. A middle-aged waitress, who looked like she'd experienced hardships, too, walked between the tables, smiling at the customers and making small talk as she poured coffee. At that moment, I would have traded my life for hers. No matter how much money I came from, how big our house was or what a good family I had, right now I would rather be in her shoes.

She caught my eye as I peered sheepishly through the window. Without shoes, bloody and wet, I looked a mess. I was 16 years old and stuck somewhere within the depths of the slums of Detroit, somewhere between late night and early morning.

Opening the door, she gave me a sympathetic look. "Can I help you?"

"No, I don't have any money. I'm OK," I stated proudly as I had been taught.

"Let me know if you change your mind," she replied.

I sat on the dusty, cracked, orange cushioned bench and considered my options. I could call my parents. I needed to get home. Yet there was no way I could call home. Then my parents would finally know. My family's lives would be in jeopardy.

A black car pulled up to the motel and I shrank down in the cushions. But it wasn't them. I resolved to call home. I motioned to the waitress and she came back out to the lobby.

"Could I borrow a dime? I need to make a phone call."

She nodded and pulled a coin from her apron pocket. She returned to her customers as I slid the dime into the lobby pay phone. My heart thundered as my shaking fingers pushed the numbers to my house. *What time was it?* As the number rang, I held my breath. A recorded message came on saying that I needed to first dial the area code. *Where was I?* My dime came back out. I had to make a collect call.

I gave the operator my home number. It rang once, twice, three times. I became more frightened with each ring of the phone. My dad would be would be furious.

"Hello?" A man's voice groggily answered.

I slammed down the receiver before the operator could give him my name. I couldn't do this. Not after what I had just gone through. Not both in the same night. To endure torture, and then disappoint the people who cared about me the most and put them in danger was more than

I could bear. I rested my head on the side of the pay phone and cried.

Glancing up, I noticed the waitress watching me and talking on the phone inside the restaurant. *Now what?*

While I silently prayed, a police car pulled up outside the motel restaurant. The officer got out of the cruiser, walked up to the door and looked at me. I didn't know whether to be relieved or scared. I had never had dealings with police officers. Perhaps he could drop me off at home.

"What seems to be the problem here?"

"I need to get home," I answered. "Can you give me a ride?"

"How old are you? Do your parents know you're out this late? Where do you live?"

I shrunk back from the pummeling questions. "Um, I'm sixteen. I live in Birmingham. Could you just give me a ride?"

"Let's talk in the car on the way home," he answered.

I agreed. *This just might work.* He spoke with the waitress again and then talked on his walkie-talkie. The longer I waited, the more exhausted I became. It was a long time since I'd slept.

"Can you tell me what happened back there?" the officer asked as he drove. "Why are you all the way out here?"

I pretended to sleep, occasionally mumbling an "I don't know," to pacify him. I could barely move the muscles of my mouth to respond. In shock, I worried about getting inside the house and into my own bed without anyone knowing. All I wanted was to get in the hot, soothing bath and soak away the aches, hurts, the blood, and the awful odor of the cologne and body fluids of so many disgusting men.

"Who took you all there way here and left you? I really need you to tell me. Are you hurt? Do you want to go to the hospital?"

Like I learned to do at the counselor appointments, I remained silent. *They can't do anything if I don't answer. All I want is to go home.*

It was a long ride before the police cruiser pulled into my driveway. The big white pillars, looked familiar yet ominous.

I quickly got out. "Thanks for the ride," I said and hurried to the front door.

He turned off the car and followed me. The front porch lights were on. Oh no. *How was I going get out of this one?*

I opened the door and my parents met me, clad in their pajamas, robes, and dark frowns. My puppy ran into my arms. I gingerly bent to pick him up. "Oh, Bowzer!" I held him tightly as he licked my swollen face. His unconditional love was a balm for my body and soul.

"Stay here while we talk to the officer," my father stated.

They went into the living room as I waited for what seemed an eternity. *How could I continue to protect my family if the truth came out? Daniel said these guys meant business. Maybe I should have taken Jonathan's offer, to keep my family safe. What would they do now that the police were involved? I was sure they were watching. How could I continue to do this without my family getting hurt?*

I recalled the string of dead animals that had shown up in our mailbox since the manipulation had begun 18 months ago. My brothers were often followed home from school. Holding my puppy, I knew that the truth wasn't an option. My dad was traveling to the east coast on Monday for two weeks.

"Theresa," my father summoned me to the living room. My parents believed that I had been out all night whoring around with boys. Their minds were made up. Nothing I said would change it without putting us all in grave danger.

The officer studied me with knowing eyes.

"May I talk with Theresa, alone?" the officer asked.

My parents went to the kitchen to make coffee. Day was dawning.

"Theresa, I know what happened," he said gently. "I've seen this before. You're not the only one. I know you're not doing this voluntarily, like your parents think." He leaned forward. "Am I right?"

I gave him the slightest indication of a nod.

"I can help," he offered, "but I need your help. We believe there is a large criminal ring involving a large group of Chaldeans. Does the last name *Gerard* sound familiar?"

My heart dropped into my stomach and my eyes widened. I stared into his eyes, not nodding or denying.

"That's what I thought." He pulled out a business card and handed it to me. "Take my card and call me when you're ready to talk. I need an insider in order to get to them. But you must realize that this is very dangerous."

You have no idea.

"We want to get the top guy," he continued. "Jonathan."

My eyes widened at his name and I swallowed. Memories of our one and only meeting flooded back.

Noting my reaction, the officer nodded and left.

Zombie-like, I went upstairs, filled the tub with scalding hot water and stayed there for hours. My tears flowed like the water faucet as I attempted to wash only God knew what from my body.

I missed school that day. Surprisingly, I was allowed to sleep all day. My mind, body, and soul screamed inside. Each time I woke, often from the pain, I closed my eyes again preferring sleep to the harshness of reality.

Late that afternoon, my brother's yelling woke me.

My mom knocked on my bedroom door. "Do you have Bowzer in there with you, Theresa?"

"No."

"Get up and help us look for him. We can't find him."

My three brothers and I combed the neighborhood, the subdivision, and the park. We made posters and hung them everywhere. The boys rode their bikes to the grocery store on the busy intersection. Allen wanted to stop by the police headquarters to give them a poster. I stalled. I knew I was being watched. If I was seen going in the police building, someone might think I was going to them for help for a different matter. I stood outside, waiting for my brothers to come back out.

Late that night, my private phone line rang. When I answered I heard a dog bark and a gunshot.

I went to my desk, opened the drawer and took out the policeman's business card. I read the name on the card, then tore it to shreds. I cried myself to sleep, knowing that even though I kept my mouth shut, the danger wasn't over. I couldn't even protect my dog.

20.
Not a Game

After the police incident, I was grounded for a long time. It was ironic to be punished at home, but I didn't argue. I was relieved to hide in my room after school, trying to heal.

I listened to my records over and over again. The Carpenters when I felt desperate, Air Supply when I missed Jim, REO when I dreamed to be normal, and ACDC when I allowed myself to be angry. I cried, wrote in my diary, and prayed. I prayed I wouldn't be called at night, now unable to get out of the house. I prayed this torture would end and I could be a normal teenage girl.

A few days later, as I was falling asleep, the phone rang. My heart stopped.

"Hello?" I said, tentatively.

"Theresa? This is Jonathan."

I froze, unable to answer.

"How are you feeling? I heard about what happened last week."

What was I supposed to say?

"I could have protected you. You didn't have to go through all of that," he said. "If you agree to my conditions, I will guarantee things like that won't happen. You will be treated like a queen and I will personally select the people." He paused. "Theresa, those guys are dangerous. You might not live through this."

I had no words to respond.

"I can make your life easier. You'll have your own nice little apartment, designer clothes, and all the money you could ask for."

"I don't know," I stammered.

"I'll get the pictures from Nick and make sure your family is protected. Think about it."

The phone went dead.

Stunned, I held the receiver in my hand for several minutes. Here was a way out, but it wasn't really a way out. It was getting in deeper. On one hand, it seemed like I would be released from having to perform various sex acts with Nick and his men. I would no longer be indebted and scared that my family would be harmed.

But on the other hand, I would be forced to leave my family, run away, and be at someone's complete will, never knowing what was going to happen. My dreams for college and a normal life would never be realized.

How would I escape this? Would Nick ever give up the photos? Ever give up his hold on me and the money he was making with me? My dad was up for another promotion. That meant a raise and relocation. Every two years it came. He also had co-workers who were told this was where they would stay. If he got that call, I would be stuck here and then what?

I couldn't last much longer. Emotionally and physically I was at the end of my ability to cope. I wouldn't live long if this continued. I had two options. Stay with the current arrangement and hope we relocated soon. Or accept Jonathan's proposition. Either way, I couldn't endanger my family.

Unable to concentrate in school the next day, I pondered the options. How would I stay alive? My parents were watching me as well as the Arabs. Should I submit to Jonathan? Hand over my life, what was left of it?

The phone rang during dinner the next night. My dad was supposed to be out of town but the trip had been cancelled. My parents didn't allow phone calls during dinner and my father was not happy about having to leave his meal and get up to answer the phone.

"Hello?" He frowned. "Hello? Hello?" He hung up and returned to the table.

"Who was that?" mother asked.

"I don't know. They hung up. But there was weird music in the background." he said.

We resumed eating dinner. But I had lost my appetite. I knew it was a warning.

21.
Home Life

Each time I ignored the telephone when it rang in the night, a dead bird or dead mouse, or a black rose was left in our mailbox. A car sat outside my house for hours after following my brother and me as we walked home from school. The warning was clear and it was deadly.

People say they wish to be rich and live in a large home. I knew that the people living in those places can be miserable. My parents fought more than ever and I was afraid they were going to divorce. My dad stayed out late and my mom was unhappy.

One afternoon, my brother was not at our accustomed meeting spot to walk home with me. He was supposed to wait for me and I was angry that he hadn't. Maybe he went home sick from school, I reasoned. I liked his company, it made me feel safe even though I knew he couldn't do anything to help. Not really.

At home, I got a snack and sat down to watch television.

"Theresa," my mom called from the laundry room. "Where's your brother?"

"I thought he was here already. He didn't walk home with me."

"He didn't come home early. He left a note that he was staying after school. But he should be home by now. Check his room and see if he is there."

His bed was made and his room was neat like he always kept it, but Allen wasn't in his room.

"No, mom," I called down the stairs. "He's not here."

She drove to the school to see if she could find him while I waited for my other brothers to arrive home from school. The three of us rode our bikes around the neighborhood, searching for Allen at the park down the street.

My mom phoned my dad who was out of town on business. She called the police. After our dog disappeared, my parents were suspicious of the neighbors. I wondered if this was another warning from the

Chaldeans. I thought back over the week, had I answered the phone every time? Would they take my brother now, too?

I was growing more terrified by the moment, but for different reasons than my mother. My brother was fragile and sensitive. He couldn't handle what I had experienced. I didn't doubt for a moment that these monsters would sexually abuse my brother just as they had done to me.

I needed to protect him. No matter what it cost me.

I had to reach Daniel and keep this from my parents. But how? I had never called Daniel.

They always called me. I didn't even have his phone number. The phone book was no help, there were two dozen listings for that last name. I searched the listings until I found one that matched the name of his street as I'd noted it in the early hours of the morning as he took me home.

I dialed the number. "Hello? Hello?" I said when the line picked up.

"Ya? Ya?" The older female had a thick accent.

"Can I speak to Daniel?"

The woman babbled in Arabic.

"Daniel, please!" I shouted into the phone. The line went dead.

Then I heard shouting from Allen's room.

"I found a letter," my mom told us. "In a notebook on his desk."

"What does it say?" I asked.

She read the letter that said Allen was unhappy about how people were treating him. He was running away to visit his Godmother in California, a thousand miles away. My mom called my dad, her friend, and our uncle who lived nearby. They talked to the police about where Allen was headed.

My mind raced. I was relieved my brother had not been kidnapped, but the situation confirmed that I still needed to protect my family. They couldn't handle my drama right now, too. I had to remain quiet and endure my nightmare until I figured some way out.

Allen was gone several days before we located him and got to talk to him. My family was a mess. And I was determined not to add to their problems.

22.
Paying My Final Dues

Typing was my last class of the school day. The teacher handed out a paper to copy on our individual typewriters. The room was silent except for the hypnotic sound of keys hitting paper. No conversations, just kids concentrating on fingering, letters, and paper.

The class was located in the same hallway as my locker. Randy, a cute Jewish boy whose locker was next to mine, was standing there. He was popular, smart, handsome, and rich, and we often joked around. With my back to the hall, pulling out my notebook, I heard something change in Randy's voice. I looked over at him. Randy stood frozen. Then I turned and saw Nick and his cousin.

"Get lost, kid." Nick looked threateningly at Randy.

Randy looked at me apologetically, and then ran down the hall to class as the bell rang.

"I have to get to class," I pleaded. "I can't be late."

"Do you really think we care, Theresa?" Nick stepped closer. "We need you after school for something very special."

"I can't Nick. My mom is expecting me home right after school."

"It wasn't a request." He backed me against my locker. "Be there."

As he reached for my throat, the typing classroom door opened and the teacher peeked out.

"Theresa, are you coming?"

"Yeah…"

"She'll be there when I'm finished with her." Nick stepped toward her. She stared at him, nodded her head, and went back into the classroom.

Nick and his cousin left, laughing down the hall.

In class, the teacher avoided looking at me. I realized she was also afraid of Nick. The teacher never spoke to me again for the rest of the school year.

****

After class, I wasn't surprised to see Daniel waiting by my locker. Randy returned to his locker but didn't look my way. Our joking around was long gone. I followed Daniel to the parking lot.

As we neared his car, I saw my friend Janie near a fancy car with an older Chaldean guy. I recognized him. He was the man with the knife who raped me. He gave me an evil smile. Janie, had been flirting with him, and hurriedly turned away when she saw me watching.

No, no. Not her too.

Seated in Daniel's Trans Am, I began, "I can't do this anymore. This is the last time."

"I know," he said sadly. "I don't know how you have survived this long."

"They can give the pictures to my parents. I don't care."

"OK. I will ask them again."

"Tell them. This is it. No more. I want the pictures. I've done more than enough to earn them, Daniel."

"I might finally be able to convince them."

We drove to a part of Detroit I had never been to before. This was an upper class neighborhood. In the middle of the night, we usually went to Daniel's family home. After school, it was usually to unknown, unfamiliar places.

I remembered my dog that I would never get back.

Daniel parked. He seemed more apprehensive than usual. The driveway was full of cars.

I reached for the door handle, ready to get this over and never do it again. Daniel laid his hand on my arm.

"Theresa," he cautioned. "Be careful. These aren't nice guys. They aren't like the others."

Daniel held my hand and led me through the garage and into the house. He held up a hand, indicating the need to be quiet as we entered the kitchen. He peeked around the corner and motioned me forward. We made our way down steep stairs to a finished basement. A den of desire.

The main room was a bedroom, complete with a large bed in the center and mirrors lining the walls and ceiling. In a separate room were low couches and a television. This room was filled with men.

Loud music played as the men watched Arabic television, smoked, and drank. I sensed immediately that this was a scary situation. I was grateful that Daniel was with me, something they hadn't let him do lately.

No one acknowledged my presence. I was nothing. An accessory or ornament. I meant nothing. I wasn't considered human.

Nick appeared in front of me. "Finally. We have been waiting for you. You're going to really like this."

"Gentlemen," he raised his voice to the room. "This is a small token of our appreciation for all your hard work. Enjoy any way you wish."

I nudged Daniel.

"Nick, she wants the pictures," Daniel said. "She feels she has done enough." Neither firm nor convincing, Daniel eyed his cousin.

"Let's see how she does today."

There was a glimmer of hope I'd not seen before. *Did Janie have anything to do with this? Perhaps she was being prepped to take my place.*

I was surprised that Daniel's quiet cousin started off first. He had only taken me twice in the past two years. He usually sat in the corner and enjoyed watching. More handsome and clean cut than Nick, he was quiet but when he did speak it was evil. The two were inseparable.

He stood first and pointed to the bed. He took me on the bed while some men watched television in the adjoining room and others drank and smoked, leaning next to the bed. Watching.

In the beginning, he was gentle. He told me to do something, tricking me in Arabic. I understood a few words and obeyed the first command. But I didn't understand the second foreign request.

He slapped my face and the men in the room erupted in laughter.

"I told you what to do," he demanded. "Now listen or there will be more."

When the cousin saw me look to Daniel, he grabbed my legs and brutally pulled them open. After he finished, I wanted to curl into a ball and recover. Immediately the next man left the television, took off his clothes and ordered me to get on my knees. This went on for hours.

Daniel stayed in a corner, watching. I knew enough Arabic to know the men teased him. I wondered if Daniel even cared about me. My hell was the loss of my soul as well as the repeated physical abuse.

When I thought they were finally finished, when I could barely focus, barely remember what I had come for, a course and uncultured Chaldean man stepped forward. Huge and sloppy, he demanded, "Stand up!" The other men were suddenly interested in the big man with me. His proceeded to order me to commit an oral sexual act on him—and I obeyed as the other Arabs wandered into the room to laugh mockingly at this spectacle.

Disgusted at what I was being forced to and tired from brutal physical and sexual abuse, I reached my breaking point. At the point of tears and struggling to breathe, I vomited all over this grotesque man.

Angry at what I had done, the man threw me to the side of the room and kicked me in the stomach. Landing hard on the floor, my head hit the wooden dresser. The men's mocking laughter filled the room. Then he kicked me again. Over and over, he kicked me, until, huddled in a fetal position, I no longer moved. Bored, the men returned to their drinks and the television.

Finally, the ordeal was over.

Daniel cleaned me up and helped me dress. My abdomen ached and I could barely stand. Nick approached. "You earned this today." Laughing, he threw a photo at my feet.

I don't remember the ride home. But I do remember clutching the picture in my hand. Holding it close to my chest, cherishing the prized possession so dearly that I bought with my body and soul.

Back home, I ran a hot bath. Washing off the fluids of other people from my body. Thankful to be home. Thankful to be alive. And thankful to have a photo.

23.
Farewell Dinner

Late one Friday evening in the spring of 1982, my dad returned overly happy from a long business trip. Usually my mom was annoyed with him when he was like this but she was happy, too. It had been along time since anyone in our home had been happy.

My brothers gathered in my room, where we played the record player loudly. The Carpenters were followed by *Grease* while we pretended we were all getting along for a change.

"What do you think is up?" I asked.

"Maybe we're moving again," one suggested.

"We couldn't be that lucky," I retorted.

At dinner Dad announced that tomorrow we would go out for dinner at a fancy restaurant. "Cancel any plans you have for Saturday and wear something nice," he said.

On Saturday, we loaded up in the van and headed off for a long drive. All the way there, my brothers and I tried to guess where we were going.

"Have we been there before?" I asked.

"Will you give us a clue?" my brother asked.

"Tell us where we're going!"

"No. No. No," our parents answered each time.

We arrived at a beautiful mansion that served as a restaurant. Our old van looked out of place among the Lamborghinis and Mercedes. Shyly, my brothers and I followed my parents inside, feeling uncomfortable yet excited to see the exclusive, upscale restaurant. We were seated and had our own personal table butler. My younger brothers enjoyed sipping their water and watching the butler refill the glass after each sip. Servers brushed bread crumbs off the table with a knife onto a small china plate.

"Order whatever you want," Dad told us.

"I want a cheeseburger," my youngest brother declared.

"When we go to fast food, you ask for shrimp," Allen observed. "Now we're at a nice restaurant and you want a cheeseburger?"

Everyone laughed. It felt good to laugh.

When our meal was nearly finished and we had sufficiently irritated the butler, my dad cleared his voice.

"I have some very important news."

"We know, dad, what is it?" I asked impatiently.

"Yeah, Dad," my brother piped up. "Tell us."

"Who knows how to spell Connecticut?" he asked.

Each of us took a turn but didn't get it correct.

"We can't live in a place you can't spell, can we?" Dad said.

We stared at each other, dumfounded. This would be my ninth move by age 17. As the news sunk in, all eyes were on me. What would my reaction be?

"Great!" I grinned. "How soon can we go?"

My family stared at me, incredulous.

"Are you sure, Theresa?" Mom leaned forward. "This means you would have to leave in your senior year."

"It's a really good move for me," Dad hastened to add. "It means moving to the company's headquarters. We'll be near New York City and the beach."

"Dad, really, I can't wait to go." I glanced around the table at each of my family members. "I've moved before, we are experts at it, right? This will be great!"

Surprised, everyone was silent for a moment. Then they all began talking at once. As my dad went on and on about the opportunities on the east coast, the many things we could do and see, my thoughts drifted off.

I'll finally get out of this. It was a do or die situation now. This is my chance to get away! I can finally be free from the years of torture! Maybe I had a chance at this life after all. And my family would never need to know what I went through for them. I just wish we still had my dog, Bowzer.

That night when the phone rang after dark, I didn't answer it. Knowing my days of torture were numbered and freedom was near, I stood up for myself.

24.
Freedom at the Price of Another

I woke up feeling *whole* the next morning. I was energized with the knowledge that we were moving far away from here. I was finally going to be free. Instead of the usual empty feeling I had lived with for years, I was determined to stop this. And I felt as if I could succeed.

I was weary of the daily terror and blackmail. I no longer cared if my parents found out. I didn't care any more if my captors carried out the numerous threats they had held over my head. Maybe I really could go to the police.

To cope, to survive the unending horrific demands, I had closed down my emotions. That morning, as I studied my reflection in the mirror, I realized I had been living in a zombie-like numbness. Going to school, walking through the motions of my daily life, friends, and a long distance boyfriend. Wondering every day if I would be summoned to perform, where I would be taken. As I brushed my teeth each morning, getting ready for the school I dreaded, I searched for an excuse to get out of what may come that day.

But today was different. I would stop it today. Whatever the cost, it would be the last day. But first I had to take care of some business. I needed to make sure someone else was protected and wouldn't be hurt by my leaving. With my shoulders straight for a change, I walked to school with my brother. Feeling closer to him than ever, I swallowed against a lump in my throat.

I got through the first period without incident. The second and third came and went.

"Guess what," I said to my friends at lunch. "We're moving at the end of the school year."

"Where are you going?"

"I'm not really sure. It's my dad's headquarters. Out east somewhere."

They weren't surprised. They knew how this worked. They were sad, but not devastated. Our relationships were pretty superficial. I asked them for their addresses and told them I would write when we got settled. They seemed to accept that lie.

I had sociology class with my friend Janie. I waited anxiously all day to talk to her alone. I'd noticed an increased number of Chaldeans around her. I suspected that she was the reason why things were quieter for me. I hadn't been called since the vomiting incident. Perhaps they were priming her to take my place.

The thought disgusted me. I *had* to protect her. I couldn't let this happen to another person.

"Janie, what are you doing after school?"

"I have plans," she hedged. "Why?"

"Wanna come to my house and hang out?"

"I can't. My mom is at work and I have to watch my little brother when he gets home from school," she said. "But you can come to my house."

"Great. I'll walk with you."

Shy and quiet, Janie was a sweet kid. I liked to do things with her. She wasn't as wealthy as we were, and because her parents were divorcing, her mom had to work full-time. Janie watched her brother after school. Though she was plain, she had a nice body. Unaccustomed to male attention, she hadn't ever had a boyfriend. With her father gone and her mom working full-time, she had little supervision. Janie was vulnerable. The perfect prey for the Chaldeans.

As we walked to her house after school, making small talk, she kept looking over her shoulder.

At her house, we ate junk food and listened to records. It was nice to laugh again like a normal teenager. For me the pressure was off. I was leaving this place soon.

"Are you dating anyone?" I asked. "The Chaldean I saw you with last week?"

"So what if I am?"

"Janie! I can't believe it. Not you! Please be careful!" I pleaded. "You don't know what you're getting yourself into. They are very dangerous!"

"You're wrong, Theresa," she argued. "He loves me. He wouldn't hurt me. He will protect me from the others. He told me."

"Janie, these guys make you do things you don't want to. They will hurt you – "

She stood. "You should go, Theresa. They warned me that you might try to convince me not to go out with him. That you would say things to me. I am not even supposed to talk to you."

"Oh, Janie," I groaned. "They will suck you in. They will hold something over your head so you – "

She opened the door. "Good-bye, Theresa."

I walked home in despair. Janie was already getting involved with the Chaldeans and had no idea what her future held. I longed to keep her from my same fate. I telephoned her many times after that. I tried to talk to her in class. I wrote her notes during school but she wouldn't read them.

It crushed me to watch her get into his car after school, knowing what was happening to her. As the weeks progressed, I watched her spirit shrivel and die. I tried to save her the way I wished someone had tried to save me. I was leaving soon, but she would be stuck here.

My nightmare had become hers.

25.
Betrayal

Alone in my bedroom, I wouldn't allow my thoughts to settle on Daniel. Similar to a child with an abusive parent, I had intensely confusing feelings for him.

I was angry that he had started all of this. I was angry that he didn't protect me. But if I allowed myself a split second of truth, I also knew a part of me loved him. Silently he drove me to each den of sin. Though he never did anything to stop the abuse, he never abandoned me. He was there, every time I was assaulted. There in the room, he watched. Then he silently drove me home.

"After he raped you," a conference attendee once asked, "did you ever have sex with Daniel again?"

"No," I replied.

But as I drove home, the long buried memory came rushing back. I allowed it to enter, wanting to know. Ready to handle it. Or so I believed.

There was one other time.

Daniel had picked me up after school. His happy mood surprised me. Usually he appeared as sad and resolved as I was when he drove me to a strange house where strange men waited.

"I have a surprise for you, Theresa." He dropped his voice and mumbled that he wanted to make up for it all. Do something nice for me.

I was confused. A large part of me didn't want to be in this car. Didn't want to be with him, going anywhere, if I didn't have to. I just wanted to go home and sleep.

"Where are we going?" I asked.

"My cousin is letting me use his house while he is at work." Daniel smiled.

His strange behavior made me suspicious. Soon, we entered a simple, two story condominium that I had never seen before. As he led me upstairs, my stomach was in knots. Yes, I cared for him, but sex had taken on a totally different meaning for me. Especially with Chaldeans.

It was a way for people to get what they wanted. For me, sex was no longer attached to love and emotions. At 17 years old, after having sex more times than I could count, I had never had sex with someone I cared about. Terror was the only emotion for me that accompanied the base act.

I didn't know what to do. *Did I have a choice here?*

Upstairs I was relieved that there were no other people in the home. That was a first. *Why did he bring me here?*

"Theresa, sit here on the bed and I will run a bath for you. I want you to relax. I want you to be happy. I am truly sorry for all that has happened to you. It's my fault. I care about you. I always have. I've seen what you have gone through and I just want to be with you. I want you to be my girlfriend." His voice dropped to a whisper. "But you know that can never happen." Nervously, I sat on the edge of the king sized bed. From the attached bath, the sound of running water caused a flood of memories. The first time. Blood all around me.

Trying to take my mind off the fact that I would have to get naked and climb in the bath, I glanced around the room. It didn't look like a Chaldean home. It looked American with simple furnishings and neutral colors.

"I will give you privacy, Theresa," Daniel said, coming back into the room. "Enjoy the big tub. There is a surprise in there. A shaver and cream. Shave yourself totally clean. For me."

Once again, I was instructed to do something. Something that would no doubt lead to sex. Naively, I still believed people were good. I didn't want to stop believing that, though it was not a belief that was benefitting me.

Feelings of betrayal swept over me. *How dare he tell me what to do and want to have sex with me.* And yet another part of me longed to be in his arms, to feel him protect me rather than abuse me.

I was nervous during the bath. I didn't enjoy it. I did as he told me and shaved myself clean. But I didn't feel clean. I felt degraded. The whole situation felt wrong. I let the water drain from the tub and wrapped a soft towel around my body. I wanted to go home.

Daniel wasn't in the master bedroom. A green negligee was laid nicely on the bed. I stared at it.

"I'm downstairs getting some water to drink," Daniel called. "I left you a little present to make you feel good. You will be beautiful in it!"

I wanted to run back in the bathroom, lock the door, and throw up. Was this a trap? Were other men coming soon? I was nervous because I didn't know if I wanted to have sex with Daniel. I didn't know how to do it with someone I cared about. And I was shocked that he wanted me. He said he loved me, didn't he?

I did as I was instructed and put on the nightgown. Dressed in the beautiful silk and lace, I sat on the edge of the bed. Daniel returned to the room wearing only his pants. He looked comfortable, happy. He stared at me.

"Wow. You look even more beautiful than I ever imagined," he said.

My heart was in my stomach. That was the first compliment I had received in years. It completely confused me. I was torn between wanting to feel proud and wonderful, while at the same time untrusting and damaged.

"I want to take a picture," he said. "To always remember you like this. For me. You are mine!"

My heart was happy that he seemed to care for me. That he bought me this nightgown. That he wanted me. But he was doing the same thing his cousins did. Take my picture like this? Would he threaten to show it around? Suddenly the facts fell into place. He was the same as they were. No different.

What would happen if I refused? I had tried that before and always been severely punished. But he said he loved me. Maybe he wouldn't hurt me. Then reality hit me full force. Daniel had been involved all along. If I refused to do as he said, then he wouldn't be my protector any longer. I would be out there all alone with the most cruel men alive. I didn't want to take that chance. To risk losing my side kick, my confidant. It was just sex after all. I could do this.

So, that afternoon we had sex. Daniel was happy. He was caring and loving, not mean or harsh. But it didn't matter. Like always, I left my body and shut down my heart.

Afterwards, as usual, he drove me home. He had a smile on his face. He even held my hand. I pretended. I was good at pretending. I knew this would never happen again.

That night, as I soaked in my bathtub at home, as I always did afterwards, I thought long and hard. Tears streamed down my cheeks. These were different tears. Tears of betrayal. My heart ached. Had they put him up to this? Did he truly love me? Did he feel terrible about what was happening to me, or was he really behind this whole thing? Daniel had done what the others had not been able to do; he had enslaved not only my body, but my heart as well.

26.
Escape

My escape was different from most girls. But my story is different from most, too. Each of us have similarities in our stories, and each of us are unique. From different backgrounds, some of us were rich, some poor, some black, some white, some had two-parent families, others are from families that were broken and dysfunctional. Some had abusive parents, or parents that abused alcohol or drugs.

Survivors seem to be the only people who we can tell, who will accept the entire story without judgment. We endured the same hell. We experienced similar acts perpetrated on us and suffer from a deep sense of unworthiness and post traumatic stress.

We end up in the same place.

Here.

I was lucky and escaped by moving. Many aren't as lucky. Still, I kept the details vague, and was careful not to let many people know I was leaving. Most of all, I didn't want the news getting back to Nick or Daniel.

"It was really sudden. But they need my dad there next week," I lied to protect myself and my family.

I knew the importance of keeping us safe, even hundreds of miles away. My dad said that the house he had put an offer on was in negotiation because the couple was divorcing. It had to go to court first, then it would be ours. It had a built-in pool and large yard. An hour from New York City, we'd be close to the beach. My family was excited. I was excited for a completely different reason. I knew that at last my personal hell was over. This move was my ticket out. My ticket to freedom.

I had to get out of town without them suspecting, before they carried out plans for Jonathan to keep me as his personal concubine. This was a battle for my life.

With God's help, I won. I told friends I wouldn't know the address until the house was finished. I felt guilty of the lie, but our safety, my life, meant more to me than a few friends who I knew I would never see again.

The downside of moving every two years was that I became cynical. Friendships didn't mean much because they were temporary. They came and went. Nor had these people done anything to protect me when I was beaten and abused. As I learned more Arabic, I understood the plans being made in the other bedroom. Waiting, I could hear Jonathan arranging an apartment for me. Planning to cut me away from Nick's business to create his own enterprise with me. More elite. More exclusive. More money. Now that I had been primed and prepared, I was ready.

Part of me was happy to get away from Nick's violent hand. Though I'd never seen Jonathan hurt anyone physically, what he had allowed and what he was planning for me was certainly not for my benefit. There was an air around Jonathan, I felt the terror and intimidation he held over people. He embodied power and control and money. He was the head of a Chaldean mafia. I had no idea what to expect from Jonathan, but I knew his plans meant I would no longer be with my family ever again. One night I would be taken away, never to be returned by the car and driver again. I would be given a new name. A new identity. New clothing. A new environment. A new family if I performed well, did what I was supposed to, and made him lots of money. Plans were coming together fast.

Would I get into the family car and drive away behind the moving van to my dad's new job? Or would I be driven in the black Trans Am to an apartment in a strange part of town to be locked away and never see my family again?

27.
New Address

As our blue and white van pulled away from my home in Birmingham, I slouched down in the seat. I held my breath, praying no one saw me.

Many miles and hours later, when I saw the Connecticut sign, I finally allowed myself the luxury of a sigh of deep relief. I was safe. They couldn't find me because I didn't even know where we were going.

We drove into a small, gated community, old and worn from the years and salted winds. I smelled the tangy sea air as we entered the oceanside community. We passed aged rental houses that held the echoes of laughter, good times, and decades of family vacations. Nearing the house we would rent for the next three months, I heard the tide washing the beach.

Dad parked the car and I got out to stretched my sore legs. The sun warmed my hair and I smiled. Safe and sound at last. I had escaped.

As difficult as it was to escape, healing proved more difficult. The scars will last a life time as I learn to live with these gaping wounds in my heart. Every morning I woke early. Down the quiet side street, I walked past four houses, including the summer home of a famous author, and through the gate. Leaving the pavement behind, I stepped onto the sandy beach and faced the Long Island Sound waters. The waves rolled towards me, welcoming me with their song as they climbed the sand near my feet.

Like a sentry, a giant rock occupied a place on the community beach. Smooth from years of salt water tides, the rock seemed to invite me onto its high recesses. Sitting Indian style, my eyes closed, I listened. I felt the sun warm and purify my skin. And I prayed. Mostly I thanked God for allowing me to be there. The tears that rolled down my cheeks now were tears of relief. I was thankful for this opportunity to have a second chance at life. And I was sad for the young girl who was taking my place back in Detroit.

Devastated by what I had endured, I hoped I could reassemble my shattered soul and be a normal teenager once more. Could I possibly enjoy my senior year of high school harboring this secret? Could I truly put it all behind me?

I spent three months on the beach. Walking, healing, and praying. I swam with my brothers during the day, went crabbing with my family, enjoyed crab bakes back at the beach house, and read novels on the screened porch at night, the cool air brushing my neck. And I lied to myself that it was over now. I could forget and move on with the rest of my life.

By the time we left the beach community and moved into our stunning new home, I felt as if I could do this. I started school telling myself I was a good girl, I could pretend it never happened and I was still a virgin. No one ever had to know. When I met a boy in school who was sweet and had no expectations, I told him I was a virgin. He never knew any different because he never tried anything physical. It was perfect.

I rejoiced that I had escaped. I had survived the depths of hell. The healing process was underway. I was safe. My family was safe. No one knew a thing.

Until college. When it all came crashing down on me.

28.
Getting Out

Many times I've reflected on this dark part of my life. Not an incident, for incidents are a short period of time. Perhaps once, maybe twice. And then they are over. This ordeal lasted for a period of time that I cannot wholly bring my broken memory to recall. I suppose for protection of my own fragile mind.

The one thing I vividly recall is the empty feeling I had each day. I went through the motions and the facade of growing up a normal teenager during these years while privately enduring hell on earth.

I have no doubt that when the people who knew me when I was teenager read this, they will be shocked and stunned. Perhaps I should have gone into acting rather than social work. My survival depended on my ability to act as if everything was normal. To keep their secret and mine. Doing my chores, going out with friends, participating in family vacations, working my part-time job, and having a long distance boy friend. Certainly there were clues that something was amiss. My parents took me to counseling because all was not well. My teachers may have wondered why a bright student looked exhausted and was failing classes.

But how does someone begin to ask the right questions? Would I have answered truthfully? The policeman knew something of my situation, but I was too frightened to confide in him.

Would anyone have believed me if I told my secret? Even now, the truth seems unbelievable for a girl in an upper class suburb in the United States. The important thing to know is that I felt I couldn't tell anyone. I was terrified of the consequences. I believed I had no options. No choice. No free will.

That is why it is called slavery.

I was brainwashed, confident that no one would believe my story if I told. Reduced to nothing inside, I was convinced that the welfare of my beloved family rested solely on my behavior. I was without hope, happiness, or future. Left only with shame.

As I have shared my story, people often insist that I must have had a choice. Why didn't I stop the abuse?

"You could have walked away at any time, told your parents or a teacher," they say.

Did I have a choice? Perhaps. But as a terrified child, physically hurt and threatened, I didn't feel that I had a choice. And that is all that really matters. Perhaps the choice I made was to go through with it, naively believing it would be one time. I planned to return the first time with the photos in hand. I was unprepared for the depth of evil these men were capable of, nor did I imagine people would be mercilessly abusive to a young girl.

Additionally, I felt the safety of my family, and the security of my father's job was mine to protect. I planned to keep my reputation and my pride intact. Instead, I was damaged physically and emotionally.

The ability to reason and find solutions is limited in an immature young teen. What kid is equipped to deal with such adult horrors? How was I supposed to know what to do in such an overwhelming and dangerous situation? What kid makes a decision to be exploited? To be raped over and over again? To stay awake all night long, locked away in a stranger's room, being hurt and violated in secret by multiple men?

An upper middle class white girl, I thought I had good self-esteem. Certainly I had good parents who provided well for me. But people prey on others. Their practiced eye saw my weakness. I was an outsider, new in the area, and I craved more attention at home. I cared too much about what others thought of me. Some might call it co-dependent. I felt I was responsible for the well-being of my family. At the end of the day, I did what I felt I had to do to protect myself and my family. I was willing to endure the torture so that my parents didn't get the wrong impression of me, that they didn't believe something that wasn't true. So that my brothers and pets wouldn't get hurt. I couldn't handle that. It was easier to endure what I had than to see them get hurt.

Some say I was stupid. I should never have fallen for their threats. Vulnerable, my soul broken after the rape, they circled in for the attack like hungry sharks who smell blood.

29

Marks, Lies, and Unawareness

How was it possible that people were unaware that a sweet, young child from the suburbs was being sexually exploited? Why did my parents fail to see?

The cynical part of me remarks, "Ignorance is bliss." I believe a few people did know something was happening. The teachers and employees of the high school where I attended, and the mothers whose houses I visited late each night.

Being new to the area, no one knew how I acted or performed in school before moving here. No one saw the changes in my behavior. That is one of the things that made me vulnerable to the exploitation. I had no support system. No accountability. No extended family to notice changes. In those parts of town, neighbors minded their own business, refusing to interfere or pry unless something directly affected them.

The only ones who had an inkling were my brothers. Younger than me, they were children struggling with their own difficulties.

The teachers never questioned the times they saw me pulled out of class by the older Chaldeans. They allowed me to go as if I simply asked for a hall pass to use the restroom. The instructors were intimidated by the Chaldeans. Yet they were adults and I was a child. By doing nothing, turning a blind eye, they allowed themselves to be controlled by this gang, and permitted a child in their care to be hurt in ways they could never have imagined.

I dreamed that one day my typing teacher, math teacher, study hall monitor, the teacher whose class was near my locker, or the security guard would say, "Theresa, can I help you? Are you being threatened? Are they hurting you? Do you need to talk?"

Unlike an inner city school with metal detectors, this was a ritzy, high class school, where most students' fathers made lots of money. I do not blame my parents for being oblivious. But I do blame the teachers and trained school personnel who never offered to help when they observed a kid clearly being manipulated by an ethnic group. They saw me slammed against the locker, spit on, and harassed. Almost daily, they watched me leave with them.

Frequently away from campus during normal school hours, I never received a detention. Never got reprimanded for skipping class. Unlike the kid who left early to go party after school, my eyes were dull, my head was down, and I never smiled. I was the picture of dread, flanked by two Chaldean cousins as I passed the teacher in the hall.

My constant challenge was what lie I would tell my mother to explain why I wasn't home right after school. Teenagers create excuses to get out of school assignments and chores to spend time with friends. I lied to protect my family. To stay alive. I was good at it because the stakes were inordinately high.

Instead of attending the four or five track practices held each week, I often made it to only one. I told the coach I had a job and couldn't always be there. Simultaneously, I told my mom I was at track practice. Though I lived within walking distance of the school, my mother didn't come to see me practice. Nor did the coach call my parents to verify that I had a job. As long as I had a qualifying speed, I was permitted to compete in the track competitions. I only competed in home events, and I only recall my mom attending one event. Easy enough.

Babysitting after school was another excuse. No one asked for the phone number where I was, or asked to see the money I made. In reality, I was working all right, but making money for someone else.

The cousins frequently came into the fast food place where I worked, just to let me know they were there, keeping an eye on me. They called the restaurant phone number and asked for me. I got in trouble for personal calls at work, and when I answered, they didn't say a word. But they never took me from work or even directly afterwards. That was traceable. They knew my parents or the police could track what time I left.

The physical abuse left marks and bruises. "Oh, that bruise?" I would question casually. "I got that from not making it over the hurdle at track practice. Boy, did that hurt."

"My brother hit me," I'd explain away another mark. Or, "I ran into something at work."

Internal physical pain was contributed to monthly menstruation pain, or as my mom termed, growing pains. I experienced a lot of growing pains in those days. The guys were usually careful not to hit me in the face. The times Nick backhanded me, I covered the bruise with makeup. Marks on other parts of my body were hidden under clothing. If it is hot and a woman wears long sleeves, it is a pretty good indicator that she is hiding something.

When my hair was nearly pulled out to keep me still, the small bald spots were hidden under a hat or a different hair style. When my legs were torn apart to restrain me, the sore joints and muscles were invisible. Invisible like the internal memories.

Children will naturally do anything to please their parents to stay in their good graces and make them proud. Children experiencing sexual or physical abuse go to great lengths to try to please their parents. My father held a powerful position, one that meant everything to him. His company had salesmen all over the world. At the annual awards ceremony, only three were honored with the highest award of a gold ring and a trip. My father received that award twice. The second year, an emerald chip was added to his ring.

My dad traveled weekly, leaving mom to raise the four of us alone. She was the single parent of the 80's. Although she never had to worry about financial resources, she was lonely. Eventually she mingled with others and found her own interests outside of the family.

In addition to their own personal challenges, my dad was frequently required to entertain customers. Ironic that I was doing the same thing in an underground way for someone else's business. Dad took customers out to dinner, followed by drinks late into the night. My mom usually was home with us kids, but at least once a week, my parents dressed up and went out together.

Beautiful with her blonde hair, blue eyes, and shining smile, my mom glowed as she prepared for the evening, excited my Dad was home and happy for a night out without the kids. We knew they wouldn't be home until the early morning hours.

As one of my brothers described, "They led their own lives, and we were along for the ride." Baggage I suppose. They loved us, but were distracted by climbing the social ladder, maintaining the big house in the right neighborhood, two cars, and yearly camping vacations.

My siblings believed we did an inordinate amount of chores compared to most kids. At least it seemed like it to us. My parents were not affectionate or emotionally attached. They were functional parents who believed in family and a strong work ethic. It was all part of the equation that added up to a good kid from the suburbs being exploited by gang members. Most people didn't realize, but there were those who suspected something and chose not to do anything about it.

Right or wrong, it is what it is. I can not change it. I am the woman I am today because I met the devil and lived in hell. Having experienced both the dark and the light, I prefer to live in the light. I choose to use my past as a stepping stone for something good. I choose not to be quiet. I want to help save another young girl from being tied up and taken against her will until she loses consciousness. To help give meaning to the pain I endured, the lies I had to tell, and the invisible marks I suffered.

30

Allen's Story

by Allen, Theresa's brother

I was the younger brother who followed my big sister everywhere. Almost two years apart in age, I wanted to be with my big sister every waking moment.

"Get me a drink of water," she said when she didn't want me around. She would send me on an errand to the kitchen. "Get me a snack from the refrigerator."

I always obliged. I wanted to be important to her, the way she was to me. When I was eight, I showed Theresa I loved her by scaring her. To get a reaction, I'd hide under her bed and hiss like a snake. She'd run screaming down the hall until she figured out it was just her pesky little brother. When she came back into the room, I'd take off running.

As we grew, we slowly drifted apart. She was a girl. I was a boy. She liked to do girl things, and I was into boy things. When we attended the same junior high school and high school, she gave me the talk.

"When we're at school, don't talk to me. I have my friends," she said.

Having outgrown the stage of grossing her out with slime and squirting her with silly string, I looked forward to being at the same school with her.

By the time we moved to Birmingham, I had attended five elementary schools and two junior highs. I would go on to attend three high schools and move across country in the middle of my senior year. But for now we were in Birmingham, probably for a couple years. Our folks promised the moving would stop, but Dad's career was the focus of his life. I rarely saw him, and when I did, he'd be reading the newspaper or watching television with a drink in hand. His job was stressful, and a lot was expected of him so his family picked up the slack by missing him at dinners, and during week-long business trips. He came from an era where the man's job was to provide for the family, and the woman's job was to raise the kids.

Dad should've read the manual on mom before he married her. Mom was not a woman to sit idly by just raising the kids. Growing up with one sister and six brothers, my mom had a zest for life and wanted to experience everything.

Each move had challenges, but my mom supported her husband. Every place we lived, my mom made it an adventure. The older we got, the less time we spent as a family. Today we all live in different states, hundreds of miles from one another.

By the time we arrived in Birmingham, my mom was raising two teens, and 11- and 9-year-old boys. She called herself mom and dad. She answered our questions about sex and relationships, and made sure we all could cook. We still poke fun at Theresa for biscuits that were supposed to be plump and ended up flying across the dining room like UFOs. How she survived three younger brothers is another story.

When we moved to Birmingham, all the fun and games stopped. A dark heaviness settled over our family. My parents attributed the dark mood to teenage hormones. In retrospect, I realize it was a spiritual darkness.

My first memory of interacting with the Chaldeans happened when I was in eighth grade. A boy told me that if I didn't do what he said, he would have his cousins hurt my sister.

"Your sister is their property," he said.

Shy and introverted, I was picked on incessantly. Even the nerds picked on me. But this one time, I fought back. This was about my sister.

"Bite me, dirt bag," I said to the overweight boy antagonizing me.

"Your sister is gonna get it now," he threatened.

That evening I mentioned what he said to Theresa. The color drained from her face.

The next day the overweight Chaldean apologized.

"I made it up," he said.

I knew he was lying.

By ninth grade I had racked up many encounters with Chaldeans, both at junior high and high school. The white kids stayed away from them. Teachers pretended not to see anything that involved a Chaldean.

There was an unwritten code everyone lived by, though I didn't understand why.

In high school, I took my first theater class and fell in love. I was meant for the stage. Soon it was the center of my life. The theater was also the one place where the Chaldeans didn't follow me. For several months I was followed in the school halls and home from school by Chaldeans.

Theresa told me to take a different route home every day. At first I figured she didn't want to be seen with me. But I saw how the Chaldean boys sneered at her. It made my skin crawl. The only one I liked was Daniel because I knew Theresa liked him.

One day I was standing by the school bookstore and Daniel's sister came up to me. She was beautiful.

"Hi," she said.

"Hi," I answered shyly.

"You're cute."

I was speechless, which made her smile.

"I like you," she continued. "So I'm going to tell you something. Be careful of my cousins."

"Your cousins?"

"They're hurting your sister," she confided.

Suddenly her sisters and female cousins moved around her like the Secret Service covering for the President.

"The cousins will not like you talking to a white boy," a female cousin said.

The male cousins clustered behind me, hemming me in. They began shouting in their language.

"Why is it OK for you to be with white girls," Daniel's sister shouted defiantly, "but we cannot like white boys?"

"You should not say such things," one of her female cousins scolded.

"Shut up," ordered a male cousin. "You don't know what you are talking about."

Students crowded around to see what the commotion was about. I felt like a sardine packed between kids in the hall. Daniel caught my eye and nodded for me to leave quickly. I slipped away to get out of the bullying cousins' sight. I ducked into typing class and took my seat. Looking up, I saw two of the cousins stop at the open doorway. They stood and stared at me for a long, uncomfortable time. Then they disappeared.

A few days later a new student came to my theater class. Chaldeans did not take theater class, and especially not seniors. Though I was a freshman, he wanted to be in my group. The guy was nice, and since I had few friends, I welcomed his company. I told my family at dinner that there was a new guy in my theater class.

"His name is Nick," I told them.

But Nick turned from nice to mean. He demanded to have the lead role in our group.

"No," I stated. "That's my role."

He pushed me out the back door into a dead end hallway. "If you don't let me be the lead," he said, "I will make sure your sister gets hurt."

I thought he was bluffing. "Go ahead," I dared. "Hurt her. But the lead is still mine."

After that encounter with Nick, I noticed a change in Theresa. No longer the bubbly, life of the party, fun loving sister, she was solemn and withdrawn. Mom said it was Theresa's PMS time, so initially I chalked it up to hormones. But this was different.

The next time class met, I told Nick he could have the lead. He took it, and failed miserably. The next play we did, Nick wanted the lead again. The teacher said it was someone else's turn, and I would be the lead actor.

Nick had another discussion with me in the dead end hallway.

"Don't hurt my sister. You can hit me, hurt me, do whatever, but leave Theresa alone," I pleaded.

He laughed. If the devil had ever come in human form, Nick was it.

On the way home from school one day, Theresa told me to take a different route. You're not my boss, I thought. I left a few minutes after her and held back. I didn't want her to see me. She had been moody and

I didn't want to suffer her wrath.

Up ahead, I saw a car pull to the side of the street alongside Theresa. I watched her get into the car and the car sped away. Though it was unusual for Theresa to get into someone's car; I assumed it was one of her girlfriends.

That evening, Theresa's mood was extremely foul. She was making dinner for the boys because our mom was at play rehearsal.

"Allen," Theresa bellowed, "set the table for dinner."

"No," I stated. "That's your job."

"You do this right now or I'm going to tell Mom," she shouted.

I turned and walked upstairs. In my bedroom, I could hear her slamming dishes and pans. I was unaware that earlier in the afternoon I had actually seen her being abducted at knife point. I didn't think about my sister because I was too engulfed in my own problems.

During that time, kids called me "the gay boy." The night before, my mom was frustrated with me and inferred that I was gay. I was tired of the harassment at school and home. I had considered running away for a few months, and this was the night I put my plan into action.

The next morning I left home at the regular time, ditched my notebooks, and jumped on a city bus only a mile from my house. Before I knew it, I was standing in front of the Greyhound bus station. Two and a half days and a few thousand miles later, I was in Sacramento, California. No one knew where I was until I called Aunt Junie from the bus station.

"You're where?" she asked, incredulous.

"Sacramento," I said as if I was there for vacation.

That week in California, I learned that my aunt was a lesbian and I had crashed her partner's 40th birthday bash. And the kids called me gay. I was a 14-year-old boy at a party with about 50 lesbians.

By the weekend I was back home in Birmingham and unwilling to speak to my mother. My siblings were more than happy to see me home again. I was surprised they wanted me there. When Theresa was home, she was locked away in her room. The boys played together and I stayed in my room, reading.

That summer the cloud lifted briefly. We traveled on summer vacation and enjoyed being a close-knit family again. But we returned to Birmingham where the dark shadow was waiting.

That school year, the days were long and sleep was precious. Sleep became my respite from the overwhelming problems. One early morning, I was awakened by a car parking in the driveway.

The doorbell rang. I looked out my window and saw a police car in the driveway. The doorbell rang again. I heard my parents get out of bed, go downstairs, and open the front door. Quietly, I stole out of my bedroom and sat on the top step, out of sight.

A police officer was talking to my parents. His radio squawked loudly and he turned it down.

"Theresa, where the hell have you been?" demanded Dad.

I could imagine the look of contempt on Mom's face.

The officer was matter-of-fact. "Did you even know your daughter was out tonight?"

"More than likely she was out sluttin' around." That was my mom's voice.

The officer questioned my parents about their slurred speech.

"We're in our own house," Mom said. "You can't do anything about it."

"Do you realize that your daughter is in extreme danger?" the officer asked. "Theresa and I talked on the way here." I heard feet shuffle on the hardwood floor and they moved into the kitchen. Quietly, I slipped down the steps to the landing, then two more steps, and craned my neck to hear what was said.

"I have a good job," Dad stated. "We're not leaving just because an officer brings our daughter home late one night."

Footsteps. I leapt up the carpeted steps, jumped into my bed and pulled the blankets over my body. I heard the front door shut and the police car back out of the driveway. I fell asleep to the sound of water. Theresa was in the bath.

By the end of my freshman year of high school, we were on the move again. Out of the blue our father was offered a new job on the east coast, a job that was created just for him. I was excited and thankful to get out of Birmingham. There was never a move I was more relieved to make.

After the officer came to our house, I didn't see the Chaldeans as much in the halls, and Nick dropped theater class.

The morning after we learned we were moving, I ran to school to tell the few friends I had. I saw Theresa's friend, Dawn.

"Guess what? We're moving," I told her. Theresa came up behind me.

"You're moving?" Dawn looked at Theresa. "Where?"

"Conne-" I started to blurt, but Theresa's shrill voice overrode mine.

"Somewhere on the east coast." She pushed past me, closer to Dawn. "We don't really know where."

Years later, Theresa and I were both in our mid-20s. She was pregnant with her first child and I was there to support her. After dropping her husband off at college for his final exam, she turned and looked at me.

"Allen, I have something to tell you," she said. Her voice wavered. "Something happened when we lived in Birmingham."

"You don't have to say anything," I said. "I know."

dumfounded, she studied me. "How do you know?"

I recounted the policeman's visit to our house, Nick in my theater class, and the times I was followed by the Chaldeans. We sat in her black Ford Escort, and Theresa cried. It was the beginning of her journey.

Today, my sister continues on her journey, warning people that human trafficking happens to any class, any race. More than a statistic, my big sister is a strong, loving, and courageous woman. I'm proud to be her little brother.

31

When Running Is No Longer an Option

by Mike Bucy

When Theresa told me what had happened to her, not for a second did I think she was fabricating a tale. Why did she choose to tell me? She says she trusted me. With me she felt comfortable, safe, and secure. The first time she felt that way with someone since those horrific years in Michigan.

Theresa and I were in love. Our story began with a rose. As the resident assistant on check-in day at the university, I was busy helping students find the right room. I honestly didn't remember her that first day but then a single rose showed up with my name on it.

I tracked down Theresa, a bubbly lady with a pretty smile and infectious giggle. We started dating. She was loving and affectionate. However, I started noticing little things that led me to believe there was something she wasn't telling me. I had some formal training in personal observation skills as part of my RA job. I also majored in personnel issues and minored in psychology. I was a fairly good judge of character.

Theresa came from a wealthy family. Her current hometown was one of the more affluent communities in our state. I had spent most of my life with my mom, living in low to middle class. Born in Pittsburgh, I lived a few lean years in Miami before moving to Indiana. I had grown up around blacks, Hispanics, Italians, and eastern Europeans. I grew up in a mostly white community but frequently traveled to the diverse city of Chicago. I didn't see colors or cultures, only individuals.

Theresa had strong family ties. Her brothers were particularly important to her. She idolized her mother and lovingly feared her father. Theresa didn't think she was from a rich family. Once I asked how much money her dad made. Theresa had no idea. And she wasn't about to ask—it just wasn't the thing to do. To me, they were the perfect rich family.

I couldn't understand how revered and feared her dad was. He was a personable guy and we chatted when I visited her home. I knew he was a big-wig in a major American company. But I didn't understand the pecking order of the upper class. Theresa talked about Connecticut, but didn't say much about her time in Michigan.

The campus we were on was picturesque. Holding hands, we walked and talked. People passed, exchanging a gentle nod. Once in a while, Theresa grabbed my arm tighter. When I looked questioning at her, she said she felt chill or that she really loved me. I noticed that she would clutch tightly to me when we passed certain groups of men. Usually Middle Eastern men.

One night I playfully snapped my belt—and Theresa cowered in fear. After all the time we spent together, she was instantly terrified of me. That's when she told me of her unimaginable life in Michigan. She sat on the floor, looking up at me, gauging my reaction to her words. I didn't say a whole lot; what could be said? It's hard to say how long it took to recap the events. It didn't matter. All I know is that this girl had experienced unimaginable events.

Her account obviously took me by surprise. I think my reaction took her by surprise.

"I believe you," I assured. "I love you."

"Still? After know this about me?"

"I was in love with you before, so what's different now?"

I had plenty of questions. How could this happen? How could her parents not know? How did she survive?

The events she described lined up with the way she reacted to certain situations. I wasn't sure what to do for her. I encouraged her to let the university police know and I helped her see a therapist. She needed someone else to talk to, to confide in.

Her biggest stumbling block was her family.

"I think you should tell them," I said.

She shook her head. "I can't."

In the summer of 1987, we both graduated and drifted apart. For 20 years we didn't have contact with each other, though I frequently wondered how she was dealing with her ordeal. Was she leading a normal life?

Reading my 2007 university alumni magazine, I saw Theresa's name. I emailed a mutual friend, and the next day Theresa telephoned. She sounded great and shared her efforts to help others who have been in her position, and more importantly, to prevent these nasty things from happening to others.

32.
Surviving

How did you survive?" That is the first question I am asked when I tell my story at speaking engagements. People wonder how I could go to college, get married, and raise children.

Since escaping the bondage and doing deep work with a good therapist, I see that the Post Traumatic Stress Disorder actually helped me survive.

Trauma victims frequently use disassociation. They compartmentalize their lives in order to survive day to day. I recognized very early that to go on each day, day in and day out, I had to shove the pain deeply away. Become as emotionally detached as possible. If I wanted to make love to my husband, I had to bury those nightmares. If I didn't do this, I might not be able to function. At all. And if I couldn't function, then my captors won again.

I knew it wasn't healthy, it wasn't really dealing with the issue, but this coping method allowed me to survive.

College was the worst. Though my time at the beach and my calm senior year of high school allowed me time to heal my body and my soul, I hadn't come to terms with my sexual foundation. I was a virgin when I was raped. I lived two long years without the ability to say no to sex. I had no control over when a man wanted to have me.

The beginning of the junior year in college, I moved back to the Midwest. This was an opportunity to start fresh and finally get my head on straight. I was accepted as a candidate for the social work department. Instead of drinking and going to parties, I began running again. I controlled my life and memories during the day. At night, when the nightmares woke me, I ran. I knew I was tempting fate by running late at night on a college campus, but I was willing to take this risk. Scared to death, yet feeling as if nothing worse could ever happen to me in my lifetime.

I ran to a little church. Even after midnight, in the pitch dark, the door was always open.

Quietly, I slipped inside, basking in the peace and security that always welcomed me. This was the one place where I felt loved. Accepted. I prayed. I cried. Then, exhausted physically and emotionally, yet happy, satisfied, and content, I returned to the dorm and slept like a baby.

When I asked Mike to write a chapter for the revised book, I wondered what his perspective would be of the time I confessed my past to him, what he saw in my behaviors and actions during those college years. We dated during our junior and senior years of college. We were from different worlds. An only child, Mike was raised by a single mom who worked hard as a secretary. They had a comfortable life, but there were times when it wasn't easy. He was just as astonished by my family background as I was with his.

I was drawn to his self confidence. He walked the dorm hall, head held high, easily making eye contact with everyone, knowing what he wanted, and what was right. He could wear sneakers with a suit and not care what anyone thought of it. He wasn't influenced by what other people said, or by the dictates of society. Serious, driven, and level headed, he reminded me of his idol, David Letterman.

Bubbly and outgoing on the outside, I shook with fear on the inside. I forced myself to hold up my head to watch and be aware of my surroundings. To make sure I was safe and see who approached me. I conformed to the rules, a product of my upbringing, well aware of the consequences I would pay for not pleasing others. Unlike Mike, I cared too much about what others thought of me.

I was drawn to his energy. At last, here was someone I felt safe with. Someone strong enough to protect me. Ours was a comfortable, exciting relationship. We were best friends and lovers. He taught me to trust and to allow myself to be loved. The relationship allowed me to begin to survive in a healthy way.

The day I told Mike, I realized could no longer hide my past from him. I had explained away my skittishness when men walked by in the dark or in intimate situations. It was a difficult internal balance between allowing him to love me, lowering my emotional walls, while always remembering, always afraid, never fully trusting. It tore me up inside.

When the incident happened, I could no longer cover it up. It was a double-edged sword. I wanted to tell him. Was he strong enough to endure my secret? Was his love for me secure? Or would he turn and run like everyone else?

I predicted Mike would reject me. I hoped it would be easier to get over him now than to fall deeper in love and fully surrender emotionally. That was the scarier option. But if we were ever to marry, then I owed it to him to tell him. It was my baggage. And it went along for the ride with me everywhere. All the time.

I hadn't planned to tell him that afternoon. Seeing his belt fly through the air, cowering at his feet, all the trust I had for him came crashing down in the heat of a fun-loving moment. As soon as I realized my reaction, I knew the charade was over.

He was quiet. He didn't say much. He let me ramble on and on. I cried and often wasn't coherent. Speaking sometimes in one word sentences, it was the first time I was ever permitted to keep going. He held my hand, looked at me from the chair he was sitting in, and listened. I wanted to curl into a fetal position, retreat deep within myself, and never come out. I kept talking, the words spilling out, often incoherently. Waiting for him to stop me. Waiting for his eyes to move away from me in disgust. Expecting him to let go of my hand, to pull away, repulsed.

Though we decided to walk away from one another after college to pursue our careers and dreams, it was healing to know we didn't walk away from each other because of my past. The day I told Mike my story, he helped me begin the healing process. He accepted my past as *history* and loved the person I was *today*.

He encouraged me to take the first step to bring to justice the men who did this, to ask for help, and get counseling. He gave me courage to accept myself and pursue my dreams. That day, Mike empowered me and I found my strength.

The simple act of successfully telling my story, being accepted without judgment, helped me survive and heal. Too many survivors, of any travesty, are not allowed this simple gift of sharing their tale to a compassionate, accepting, listening ear.

It would be nearly 20 years before I could tell the whole story again. This time to a female friend I worked with. Over the years, I was rejected each time I started to tell it. Stopping after only a few sentences. Shut down. Rejected for a part of something that made up who I was. One of crucial pieces of myself.

Each rejection was devastating. Each time I retreated deeper inside myself. Wounded in another way. The counselor sitting across from me with a look of horror, another in shock, the stranger weeping after hearing what I physically endured. Each time I got up and walked out, never to return.

Denial is a balm. People don't want to believe this happens in our country. Let alone in our communities. They may have heard of trafficking in other parts of the world. Or perhaps within the U.S. but to girls who have been tricked and brought here from other countries like Russia and Mexico. People don't want to admit there is even a slim possibility that young American girls are forced into prostitution or exploited. Especially not girls from the suburbs. Many people have settled in the suburbs, believing it is the safest place to raise their family.

Horrified by our stories, they turn us away. Unwilling to hear the nasty details. It is too close to home. By rejecting my story, people are essentially saying that it is untrue. They reject me and they reject other girls like me. Their choice to react that way forces us to remain a victim.

Other trafficking survivors tell me of similar experiences. Too many counselors, who haven't been trained in this field, who are uneducated about human trafficking, can't help us with our much needed healing. They clearly don't know what to recommend.

So we endure alone. Medicated, and barely surviving each day. Secretly desiring a fulfilling life where our nightmares no longer affect every aspect of our lives.

Healing begins when we put a voice to our pain and what happened. Too many women who have gone through various forms of trafficking tell me that they can't fathom telling what happened to them. They can't tell their story publicly. They can't form the words. Even writing it down is extremely painful. The raw anguish eats away at them.

Telling the story makes me relive it. Brings the buried memories to the surface. Voluntarily. Making me vulnerable once again. But this is a vital component in moving from a victim to a survivor. When I use my painful experience to help others, when I enter worthy relationships and learn to trust another person, I move from survivor to victorious.

The abuse is only part of my story. Part of my life. The acceptance of another, helps me to accept myself. To accept all the parts of my history. Then I move from not merely surviving each day, but I begin to thrive.

33.
Answers

As I speak and share my story, these are the questions that typically follow:

Q: Did Jim ever find out?

A: No, Jim never really knew what happened. We never married but were reunited again when I was 34 years old. Long past being boyfriend and girlfriend, we rekindled a friendship. Reminiscing one day, the subject of the day he visited my school came up in conversation and I was prepared to tell him the truth. Since we never married, I no longer felt the pressure to be a virgin.

But when I started to tell him, he quickly interrupted.

"I don't want to know," he said gently.

"You don't?"

"I know something terrible happened back then, but I don't want to remember you differently." He paused. "Let's just leave it be. So my memory of you stays the same."

To be honest, a part of me was relieved that I didn't have to tell him and hurt him. Another part of me felt resentful that he was unable to hear it, because it was *too hard*, while I had been forced to live through it, day after day for two years.

Jim died several years ago. He never knew.

Q: Why didn't you tell your parents about the first rape?

A: Some will not understand why I chose not to tell my parents immediately about the rape.

Date rape was not a common term in the early 80's. Girls weren't educated on this in physical education class like they are now. There were no posters that read, "Just say no."

I have pondered why I didn't walk in the front door and tell my mother everything. First, I felt incredible shock at what had just happened. I felt guilty that I had disobeyed my mother's instructions and gone home with him. I was not being honest about where I was. My parents believed I was a track practice and had I been where I was supposed to be, none of this would have happened. The thought of revealing to my mother that I had been foolish, acted in direct disobedience, and suffered the worst humiliation of my life, was too much. I judged myself guilty. I perceived that it was my fault.

Secondly, there were family dynamics involved. My mother was raised a strict Catholic and ended up pregnant in the 60's. Her family pressured her to marry my dad though they were not happy about it. Begrudgingly, she became a mom and a wife. As I grew older, being her only daughter, she told me many times that I was to remain a virgin until marriage. While sex was a wonderful thing, she said, if I got pregnant, she would throw me out and I was never to return home.

When I was raped, I felt there was no way I could tell them. It would devastate them to know I was not longer a virgin; I had done precisely what she predicted and had disobeyed them. It would have crushed them. Like Adam and Eve who hid from God, I was ashamed and hid the truth from my parents. In the back of my mind, I was convinced that if the truth was revealed, I would have had to leave my family.

My parents believed a family should solve their own problems privately. If something terrible happens, it becomes a family secret and is never discussed again. I feel strongly that had I told them about the rape, they would not have called the police or filed charges against the boy. In their eyes, I would have been the guilty party and been punished as such.

Q: Did your extended family suspect a problem?

A: Our extended family lived in other states and I didn't have long-time friends since we moved so often. No support network. No one to help out when things got tough, no one to confide in, and no one to notice changes taking place in my life. These were crucial contributors that made me vulnerable. If you recall, Janie had similar vulnerabilities. Traffickers are experts at knowing who to prey upon.

Q: After you moved away, did you tell your parents what happened?

A: I do not wish for anyone who reads this book to view my parents as anything except good, providing, loving parents. For many years, it was my decision not to tell them what had happened. After we moved, it took a lot of time to recover and heal from the trauma of those long years. Looking back I realize that I suffered from Post Traumatic Stress Disorder (PTSD) after we moved away. I tried to forget and reconstruct my life. I finally had the life I wanted and was starting over.

A senior in high school, I got involved in school activities, developed a pleasant group of friends, and met a nice, shy boyfriend who was safely not physical or affectionate with me. I didn't want to mess up my new life, so I shoved the past deep inside.

Still not wanting to disappoint my parents, I went to college and did what was I thought was expected of me. After I graduated from college, I told my parents an abbreviated version of the abuse and slavery. Even as an adult, I couldn't bring myself to tell them everything. I was their little girl. I still wanted their approval. Though it no longer mattered that I wasn't a virgin, I didn't want to hurt them.

I did want to correct their misconception that I had been out "having fun with the Arabs." I tried to convince them that I wasn't acting on my own choices back then. To this day, they don't know the entire story in its horrific detail. It is difficult for us to discuss. What parent wants to believe they didn't protect their child? In my heart, I know that if they had known what was happening, they would have moved heaven and earth to save me.

Q: What happened to Janie?

A: I tried to locate Janie on a classmate location website. Perhaps she got married and changed her name. Or moved far away like I did. Perhaps she didn't survive the ordeal she most surely faced after I escaped.

Many years later, I passed through Detroit and picked up a daily newspaper. There was an article about an upper class, white girl in her early twenties who had disappeared and was later found murdered. There were rumors that she had been secretly dating an Arab or Chaldean man and I knew her fate could have been mine.

It made me think again of Janie. And wonder just how many girls were victimized in this way. The appetites of these evil men were unquenchable.

Q: How did it all end?

A: I moved to Connecticut and didn't tell any of my Detroit friends my new phone number or address. If I had remained in Michigan, I doubt I would be alive today. I suspect I was released so easily because another person had been primed to take my place. Once I was given a ride home by the police, my captors were aware that my parents and the police were more protective and watchful. I believe they found another victim to manipulate.

Q: Did you ever get all the pictures back?

A: No. I did receive two pictures in return for the years of abuse, though I have no idea how many were taken the afternoon of the first rape. There is a high probability that other photos were taken during the horrific nights and afternoons of hundreds of men taking turns.

Q: Did you see other girls? Were there other women in the same situation as yourself?

A: I never saw other girls or women during my bondage. I was delivered by myself. Men were already waiting. Alone and secluded, I was locked away while men were brought to me. It's possible that other girls were involved in different ways, in different locations, to different men.

Q: Do you think Daniel was a pawn or do you think he set you up?

A: I think he did set me up. It is extremely hard for me to contemplate this or admit it.

Q: Why do you think they let you go?

A: I think they let me go because the police were involved. They were aware that the police were suspicious. They had no idea what I told the police and weren't willing to sacrifice their entire operation and financial situation for one girl. No matter how much time they had taken to groom me, it was easier to get another girl and start all over.

Q: Are you fearful they will come after you now?

A: I realize that at any moment, they could find out that I have written this book and told my story for the world. But decades later, I am nothing to them. Perhaps their male children are now doing the same, and worse, to young girls.

Q: Do you regret telling your story and speaking out about modern day slavery?

A: Not a day goes by that I ever regret the decision to publish my story, to speak publicly, or show my face on television to tell what happened to a normal kid from the suburbs. This is my purpose. It is not easy. I battle feelings of unworthiness, and a bad book review by a stranger who isn't educated on the topic of human trafficking can be devastating. When I speak at a conference and a counselor tells me that she is working with a child who is being sexually exploited commercially, and that my story opened her eyes, then it is worth the pain.

My teenage daughter was ridiculed by some unkind acquaintances who insinuated that I am unhealthy or unclean. My daughter took it in stride, defended me, and grew stronger for it. There will always be cruel and unsupportive people who do not understand. Judgmental people. There will be family members of the opinion that I should stay quiet, protect the family name, and brush a bad experience under the rug.

Secrets lose their power when they are no longer secrets. My decision is to share this so that other people will know that human trafficking takes on many forms, happens anywhere, and can happen to any kid.

Q: How prevalent is human trafficking in the United States?

A: I regularly get calls that a teenager has been found and needs help. As word gets out and people become educated to recognize the signs, we see how prevalent this crime is. Headlines report instances frequently.

I meet with emergency and medical personnel across the nation to educate them on what to look for and how to help. These girls live a violent life. Frequently they are first seen by emergency and medical personnel. But because these caring professions don't know what they are dealing with, they patch up the girls and send them right back into it.

Q: What happened to you afterwards? Did you have a hard or easy life once it was over?

A: For the most part, I have had a relatively easy, good life after I escaped the torture. No one saved me. No one even asked if everything was OK. No one had the courage to defy the rich, powerful bullies in our school and offer me assistance.

After my escape, I dedicated my life to helping others. I went to college and became a licensed social worker. I attended graduate school where I trained as a guidance counselor. I remained a social worker, working with pregnant and parenting teens. Blessed that I escaped my horrible trial, I want to make it life easier for others.

Several years after college, I married and began a family. I made a decision that I would never let those evil men continue to own me. Though I shut away the horrible memories, they surfaced at night in my nightmares. Unfortunately, there was a great deal more damage than I realized or cared to admit. My marriage did not survive. Relationships were difficult for me. I desperately wanted a savior, a protector. Yet I never found anyone who could provide what I needed, or who accepted my dark past and emotional scars.

It has been a long journey of healing. I'm better at taking down the facade of always being strong and doing what is expected of me, while internally fighting demons. Now that the sinister secret is out in the open, I plan to live the rest of my life raising my three beautiful children, keeping them safe from harm, and helping them have high self esteem.

I want to educate society on the horrors of trafficking, and give hope and healing to those that have suffered unbearable things. For those who have been abused, I carry the message that life can get better. My goal is to help others and be a catalyst to end sexual slavery.

Slavery still exists. It needs to stop. Now.

34

The Facts about Human Trafficking

What do you think of when you hear the words slavery or human trafficking? Do you envision a little boy in India making rugs for 12 hours a day, given one small bowl of rice to eat, and paid little or nothing while he works off a debt for his family? Do you think of a young Egyptian girl sold as a maid to a rich family in another country, leaving her family only to be locked in a room day in and day out, forced to have sexual relations with the male members of the household? Do you think of children being stolen and kidnapped from their homes, forced to work on cocoa plantations?

What about a four-year-old girl in Cambodia for hire to rich tourists for sex? Or a young man told he will have a wonderful job when he leaves his poverty stricken country, only to find that he is now hopelessly indebted to the new employer for thousands of dollars for his passage?

What about a nine-year-old making soccer balls to be sold in the United States? Beaten if he does not meet an impossible quota each day?

Yes, these are common forms of slavery and trafficking that happen every day, in every country of our world. In the United States, we live in our nice, safe homes, envisioning that slavery is long gone when in reality, 27 million people are trafficked worldwide each year.[viii] Half of these are children. It doesn't just happen outside of the U.S. or in third world countries. According to the Department of Justice, estimated that 14,500-17,000 victims of human trafficking are brought into the United States each year. "It plagues the U.S. as much as it does underdeveloped nations."[ix] It happens to your neighbor. It can happen across the street.

According to Polaris Project, there are several factors that make a location susceptible to trafficking, either as a destination site or a transit site:

- proximity to a border
- extensive highway systems
- growing immigrant populations

- proximity to large universities
- international corporations
- agricultural industries
- military bases

Trafficking occurs in major cities such as Dallas, Baltimore, Atlanta, El Paso, San Diego, Los Angeles, Miami, and New York City. It also occurs in Minneapolis, Toledo, and Tampa, to name a few. The U.S. Department of Health and Human Services defines human trafficking as "(a) sex trafficking in which a commercial sex act is induced by force, fraud, or coercion, or in which the person induced to perform such act has not attained 18 years of age; or (b)the recruitment, harboring, transportation, provision, or obtaining of a person for labor or services, through the use of force, fraud or coercion for the purposes of subjection to involuntary servitude, peonage, debt bondage, or slavery."

Modern day slavery consists of many different aspects including labor and domestic slavery, debt bondage, child soldiers, child brides, organ trafficking, some international adoptions, prostitution, and sex trafficking of children and adults. Traffickers gain complete control over a person's identity or individuality through mental, physical, or emotional abuse. Sometimes all three.

The use of threats, manipulation and coercion are employed until a person submits.[x] Shared Hope International states, "Traffickers/pimps use violence and psychological manipulation to control girls and convert their bodies into cash." It is compelled service. Victims feel they must do what they are told; they feel they are unable to leave and if they attempt to run, the people they love will be severely harmed. Traffickers are experts at breaking the will of their captives. They do not function by a moral compass as their victims do. After breaking the will of the victim, they groom the victim for upcoming acts with other abusers.

A document by Shared Hope International on Domestic Minor Sex Trafficking in the United States tells a typical American girl's story. "Tanya was walking home from middle school one day when she met her first pimp. He drove up beside her in a fancy car and told her she was pretty. She was 12 years old. She was a smart kid, and taking classes for gifted and talented students. It felt good to have someone interested in her and he was sincere and had a nice smile. Every day for six months he met her after school and they talked. He bought her small gifts and she said he made her feel special. He was making an investment and crafted an illusion of trust and loyalty that bound her to him emotionally. After six months she finally agreed to get in his car.

"When the door shut, Tanya's life changed forever. Her boyfriend suddenly became her pimp. She had never left her community before, but suddenly found herself far away from home. He took away her identity and made her his slave. For the next five years, he had absolute control over her and prostituted her to over 100 men per month. She knew she couldn't run, he told her, "You're mine. I know where I got you and I can get you again." She was arrested many times and was moved from state to state. There was no place for her to run and she was without hope for rescue."

The Trafficking Victims Protection Reauthorization Act of 2005 cited the congressional finding that 100,000 to 300,000 children in the United States are at risk of commercial sexual exploitation.[xi] Dr. Richard Estes states, "Tens of thousands of U.S., Mexican, and Canadian children and youth become victims of juvenile pornography, prostitution, and trafficking every year."[xii] Researchers have confirmed that underage girls are the bulk of the victims in the commercial sex market, including pornography, stripping, escort services, and prostitution. And the U.S. Department of Justice states that the average age of entry is 12-14 years of age.

I was in the rare five percent of trafficking victims that didn't experience incestuous relations. I hadn't been physically abused at home and my parents weren't drug addicts. I was in the rare two percent who came from a family that was still intact while I was victimized.[xiii] While the majority of children at risk are youth from broken and abusive homes, the foster family system and runaways, "sexual exploitation of children is not limited to a particular racial, ethnic or socio-economic group."[xiv] The study, printed in *News Bureau* on September 10, 2001 stated, "many of these children live in secure, middle class homes and few parents are aware of their children's involvement in pornography and prostitution."[xv] Insidious and undetectable, many law enforcement officers and child welfare agencies do not realize the scope of the problem. Dr. Estes calls child sexual exploitation the most hidden form of child abuse in the U.S. and North America.[xvi]

Because traffickers aim to have complete control over someone's identity, it can potentially happen anywhere, to anyone. In reality, I *belonged* to Jonathan, though it seemed as if I belonged to Nick. Nick was the middle man. As with victims, traffickers can not be identified by specific socio-economic or racial characteristics, though it is more common among cultures that don't value women. Traffickers range from familial, mom-and-pop operations, to highly organized networks that are international business. Generally, they are organized and connected with contacts in many cities.

Experts at beating down their victim with emotional and mental abuse until they are too scared to tell anyone. Their tools include force, torture, manipulation, and coercion. Psychologically and physically, the message is the same. The victim is valueless. Worthless. Sexual slavery is about controlling people.

In his book, *New Slavery*, Kevin Bales states that it also involves an economic relationship. Though I did not realize this at the time, it certainly related to my situation. I was used as a reward and incentive for others to perform better or produce more. I was a prize for a job well done. While I was living it, I never considered the economic nature of my slavery. I didn't collect money after sex acts, and I didn't see Nick receive money from the men. It is possible that this may have taken place in the other room where the men gathered, waiting their turn.

As I entered these men-only dens, while my eyes adjusted to the smoke and darkness, I could see the coffee tables piled with drinks, cigarettes, and lots and lots of cash. It was clear, that a business transaction that had been arranged prior to my arrival. The conditions were understood by everyone except me. My role was also a business transaction between Nick (and Jonathan) and myself. I was working off the price of the pictures. As long as I was profitable to them, they worked to control me to ensure that this arrangement continued.

In addition to coercion and an economic factor, another core characteristic of slavery is violence. Bales states, "Slavery is about having or feeling as if you have no choices at all, no control over your life and a constant fear of violence."[xvii] Many victims are tricked into trafficking. Once in, the person is usually enslaved until death. Murder and suicide are the most common means of escape for most victims. The key is "loss of free will."[xviii] I felt that I had no choice but to submit, to do as I was told or be severely punished. My loved ones would be harmed or killed. And that was not an option to me.

It is extremely challenging for Americans to comprehend this topic. Most would like to turn away from it, deny it happens or re-victimize the survivor by not believing them, requiring them to prove their story, or stating they must have had a choice. Everyone in America has free will, right? This is the land of the free, right? Everyone has options and choices, right?

Unfortunately, that is not the case. Anti-human trafficking advocates bring awareness to the public about trafficking, re-educate people regarding slavery, and attempt to re-frame people's ideals regarding prostitution. It is a daunting task that often keeps us so busy trying to change the mentality of people, fighting for the voiceless to be understood, that we have little time or energy left to save the victim. But one can not be done without the other.

Lisa Thompson of the Salvation Army states it perfectly in a recent email letter posted on Dignity List-Serv, "...one article details how a young girl was violently forced into the sex trade and how she ultimately accepted her role as a prostitute and tried to attract buyers. Professionals in the field of torture, domestic violence child sexual abuse, and commercial sexual exploitation refer to this process as seasoning, grooming, and or conditioning. In 1973, Amnesty International described the coercive techniques (besides physical torture) used to gain control of political prisoners; techniques such as isolation, induced debility, exhaustion, threats, degradation, enforcing of trivial demands, and the granting of occasional indulgences, to mention a few. These are the same means (as well as physical torture) that are used to subjugate women and girls in prostitution and pornography."

The women/girls we see on the street corner may give every appearance of freely choosing to be there, while the unseen forces that condition her to be there are every bit as real as if they were made of yards of barbed wire. Moreover, if a girl in Cambodia can be conditioned into prostitution, why can't an American woman or girl? Given the conditioning that occurs, how then can any casual observer judge whether someone is a forced prostitute or a voluntary one! If someone who was forced into prostitution becomes conditioned to the life, and accepts their fate, are they now a voluntary prostitute?

Those are the facts on human trafficking from a victim's perspective. What child grows up with dreams of being a prostitute? What student checks prostitution or stripper as their desired career choice? And how many do this voluntarily? Taking home 100 percent of the revenue they made at the end of the night? The cold, hard fact is that prostitution is, in most cases, a form of human trafficking. And human trafficking has many faces. All of which are evil.

35

Spirituality Saved My Life and Soul

I believe my soul wasn't with me during the time of abuse. My soul retreated into a protection mode. This soul loss saved my life and my sanity.

Had my soul stayed and endured the years of torture, I would have been a broken person forever. I could have given in, turned my back on my family, and remained a sex slave, a full-time prostitute for the Chaldean ringleader's benefit. Until they wearied of me and replaced me with a younger, fresher girl and disposed of me physically or threw me aside with nowhere to go.

I could have ended up in a mental institution, driven crazy from the abuse, with no one to confide in. Though I felt empty, my body devoid of a soul, I also felt a protective bubble encircling my body, an energy that appeared when I was alone with my thoughts, my despair.

Always in the bath.

Showering me with love, giving me strength to endure until the ordeal was finished. I believe this energy were my angels, cleansing away any harm that had been done each day, repairing the physical, mental, and spiritual damage. Making my body whole again, even without my soul.

This energy, these angels, kept me alive. Kept me going so that I could be rejoined with my soul later, begin the healing process, have a family, and someday tell my story. This process allowed me to help others who endured some horror from which their souls temporarily retreated as well.

I felt the angels' presence but didn't realize what they had done for me until much later. Unable to find a therapist equipped to handle my story, I was doing self-therapy through journaling when I suddenly became very angry.

"How could you let this happen to me?" I demanded of God. "Where were you when I needed you? All those times, for all those years? As I lay there being abused over and over again?"

With calming clarity, I heard Him say to me, "I was right there with you, Theresa. Making sure that nothing worse happened. You could have died! You endured what I knew you could handle. When it would have been more than you could bear, I stopped it."

A wave of memories washed over me. Scene after scene, moments when I could no longer take another person climbing upon me. There would be a knock at the door, ending the abuse. The times the knife held at my throat would suddenly drop from his hands. I could have been killed, left for dead in strange, out-of-the-way places. The possibilities of being tortured beyond what had occurred flooded my mind.

It was then that I realized the significance of the baths I took after each sexual torture.

All the times I was forced to have unprotected sex with dozens, hundreds, thousands of men. Miraculously, I never became pregnant.

Why hadn't I thought of this before? I never used any protection and certainly none of the men cared enough for me or their possible children to use a condom. I was never a human being to them.

I also should have been plagued with sexually transmitted diseases. Based on the number of men who obviously were not careful with their own sexual health, my chances of being passed incurable diseases was nearly impossible to miss. The only complication I experienced is the human papilloma virus (HPV).

"My angels surrounded you during the baths," the Lord lovingly explained. "They washed away the harm your body received. Cleansing, healing you from the inside out."

Dr. Jeffery Barrows, an OB/Gyn who lectures to physicians about the medical implications of prostitution upon a woman, offers a medical explanation—at least one to explain why I didn't get pregnant. "The body can stop ovulating during traumatic events," he told me. "It is possible that this is what your body did the entire two years."

I believe in miracles. While this can be explained medically, I firmly believe that God knew the limits of what I could endure. He had a greater plan for my life.

36.
My Spiritual Foundation Paved the Way

When I was a child, each night as my mother tucked me into bed, she read to me about Catholic saints. My favorite story was about my patron saint, Teresa, the Little Flower.

The story said that on the day she died, the skies opened and rained roses. The picture showed Saint Teresa bending over the bed of a child who sweetly slept like a little cherub. The smiling saint laid a single rose in the open hand of the sleeping child. I dreamed of being worthy enough to have Saint Teresa visit me during my sleep and bless me with one of her divine flowers.

Later, in the 1980's, I watched a movie that made me ponder the intervention of the divine in my own life. In *The Seventh Sign*, a woman, portrayed by Demi Moore, was torn between her everyday struggles and her religion. She had a recurring dream. In the dream, she was confronted by a man in ancient garb, carrying a clay pot. Another kind faced young man who she was friends with, was thrown violently to the ground. Repeatedly the evil man demanded of Demi Moore, "Do you know this man?" If she publicly admitted her friendship with Jesus, acknowledging she was a Christian, she faced a tortuous death by the Romans. If she denied the truth, took the easy way out, she would turn away from His rich and unconditional friendship. By denying her faith, she would lose her soul.

I have often had this dream. A nightmare, really. What would I do in a similar position? Why was I so torn making this decision? I was confident deep in my soul that I would freely give my life for a stranger if needed. If I was confronted in a dark alley, a convenience store, or parking garage, I would have no fear of facing death if it meant jumping in front of a bullet for a stranger.

What does this have to do with slavery? I faced similar decisions daily. Whether or not to deny or tarnish my family's name. Which was the worse of two evils? Devoted to my faith, devoted to my future husband, and my church's requirement to retain my virginity, I chose my path. I was a child faced with important, life-threatening decisions.

When Saint Agnes was 13, still a child, she was faced with a similar dilemma. Yet she never floundered in her faith. She turned down jewels and riches for her promise to God. Forced to decide, she chose her faith. As a result, she spent the rest of her life in sexual slavery.

I chose my family. As a result, I endured sexual slavery. Despite the horror, I never wavered in my decision. Although others may not comprehend this, God understood. He helped me face the bonds and torture. Later He blessed me with the ability to tell this story. My experience shows others that bad things can happen to anyone. We choose our paths from the options available at that moment. And right or wrong, the Lord helps us through the results of that decision.

I prayed for Him to take away the pain. To make it stop. For some way out of this nightmare. And when the trauma was finally over, He helped me put back the pieces of my soul. When I was healthy enough, He helped me find a purpose for it.

It took years for me to realize that I do have choices. I can say no. But I was powerless during those years. But when I was released from captivity, I turned that power around and used sex to my advantage. But that extreme left me unhappy, empty, and hollow like a shell. Even on my own terms, it didn't satisfy. It took me years to realize that the physical union between two people is sacred. It is the divine knitting together of the physical and the spiritual only when it doesn't involve power. It is God's perfect design that both the man and the woman be right with God. They both surrender their power and then they are blessed with a truly spiritual experience in the merging of two into one.

37.
Seeking Help

Many years after the abuse, I sought out a therapist who could help me heal. A counselor once said, "It's not if you need a counselor, but when." For me, I needed help from someone trained in my experience.

I had gone to a few rape crisis centers, but I did not fit into their typical rape client profile. One counselor asked if she could hypnotize me. There were so many details I couldn't remember including the time line of the incidents and how long the slavery had really lasted. Nightmares haunted me night after night. I wanted to know, yet was afraid to know. Could I release the control I had constructed around my mind and surrender to the unknown? I was afraid of what my mind would do when I finally uncovered what was carefully buried. Would I have a nervous breakdown? Would I go crazy? The nightmares were bad enough but what demons would be released if I remembered all the details?

After hearing part of my story, another counselor, didn't want to hear anymore. She advised me to leave the details buried.

"Why bother to dig them up?"

She recommended that I store the bad memories away in a box in my mind. Fill the box with the ordeal, close the lid, and lock it. I didn't understand this, but it was the only advice I had received. I hoped I would be able to sleep better but was frightened that one day the box would be suddenly opened.

But locking the memories away in a Pandora's Box had the same result as in the myth. I needed to write this book, but I was afraid to open the box. Would I ruin all the hard work I had done over the years to heal? Would revealing these memories catapult me into a nervous breakdown? Or would I remain strong and capable, able to deal with the horrific memories of my past? Had I healed enough?

This was the turning point for me. If I truly was healed, than I could endure the writing of the book. As a journalistic approach to further healing, I began to write. For myself. The blank, receptive paper was a safe place to release the nightmares that plagued my mind.

As my oldest daughter neared the age when my abuse had begun, I realized that I needed to write this for others. For parents and professionals. I wanted to wake our community to the danger of not standing up for another when we know something is wrong. It is not enough to leave it to the police. Things are not always as they appear. For those who have endured their own traumatic experiences, I want to empower them, to remind them they do have options.

Writing this book was hard work. Night after night. I took long breaks from writing to mentally survive. My motive was not to publish, but to process. Going public meant revealing my carefully concealed humiliation. Several people agreed my slavery was a terrible thing for a child to live through, but it would be best if I kept quiet.

"You'll risk your safety and the safety of your children," they cautioned.

"You'll risk your reputation," said another. "You will look bad."

The irony of the last statement still surprises me. Why is my reputation spoiled because of what evil men did to me?

"Putting this horrible abuse out in public is selfish," someone said.

In his book, *Keep Going: The Art of Perseverance*, author Daniel Marshall III, a Lakota Native American wrote, "Where you are comes from the blood of those who set you on this journey. That is likewise unchangeable. What you see in the reflecting pool of truth is who you are. You cannot change that, so it is wise not to curse it. The wiser choice is to embrace it and make it your strength."

Yes, I was frightened to tell others. Yes, I was scared that I might be found again by my abusers. Yes, I was scared that my children would be hurt. But the more research I did, the more people I talked to, the more I was convinced that this was my life's mission. I needed to turn this unspeakable evil into something good.

A wall at the National Underground Railroad Freedom Center in Cincinnati reads, "If not now, then when?"

38

Parent & Professionals Section:
What Can You Do?

As long as the demand exists, our children are at risk. In my experience, there is no shortage of evil men intent on exploiting weaker young girls to gratify their selfish greed. And their desires are never satisfied.

This section is written to parents, teachers, principals, coaches, law enforcement officers, medical, and counseling professionals. I implore you; do not sit idly by. Are you afraid of losing your job if you step forward? Of angering a parent? *Don't ignore the red flags.*

As a parent, are you afraid that your actions will cause your child to cry or runaway from home?

If you have a nagging feeling that something is wrong with a child you know, if you have a hard time sleeping because you suspect something is wrong, I encourage you to trust your intuition.

How would you respond if I had been that child in your classroom?

If I had been that child in your medical office?

In your counseling office?

In your youth program?

In your immediate or extended family?

Would you make the choice to go down the hard road, with hopes of saving a child or would you ignore it? Wish it away? Turn your back?

I dreamed, wished, prayed for a person to help me. For someone to believe me. To help me. For God to send someone to rescue me.

For me, that person never showed up. Not the guidance counselor who failed to ask why my grades were falling, the principal who didn't ask why I had skipped class, the security guard in the school hallway who ignored the physical abuse I endured, the teachers who turned their back when I was being harassed, the cop who took me home after being kidnapped, drugged, and left for dead, my boyfriend who knew something was amiss, fellow students who knew I was being bullied. No one took the harder path.

God provided a way and gave me the strength to survive. The fact that I am here now to help save others is a miracle. Statistically, I should be dead, in jail, have attempted suicide, become a drug addict, or severely dysfunctional due to my past.

Parents, you have a keen sense of your child's emotions. Rely on this! Depend upon this. Do not doubt your ability for a moment. For mothers, the child spent nine months physically attached to you. During the years, you have wiped their tears, mended their hurts, nurtured them, and taught them life's lessons. When you sense trouble with your child, let nothing stand in your way of getting to the bottom of it. Be like the mother bear with her cubs when they are young. At any sign of danger or risk, claws come out, fangs are bared, and the growl is loud and fearsome, sending the worst of enemies scurrying away.

As our children grow, become stronger and independent, do not relax your guard. This is the time to have hawk eyes and finely tuned radars. Listen to the unspoken messages of the child. They still need our protection. Unlike sea turtles that lay their eggs on the beach and never interact with their young, we have our children with us longer than any other species on the planet. Our children must be protected and equipped to successfully make their way in the world.

If we don't do it, then who will?

In 2000, the American Academy of Pediatrics reported that one in five adult women have been sexually abused in their childhood. With the Internet and increase in technological communications, how do we protect our children? How do we prevent them from being exploited? There are many publications on the internet that offer suggestions on how parents can protect their child from sexual predators and molesters. Being aware and watchful is the first step.

- Ask questions, know their world, their interests.
- Know who they spend time with.
- Know where they are.
- Check to make sure they are sound asleep in their beds each night.

- Where are they going? With whom? Are they spending the night with friends and are the parents at home?
- Know the address and phone number to the place they are going. With so many teens having cell phones, parents often think they don't need another number.
- When a teen babysits, get the address and the phone number of the home where they will be.
- Take your teen to their destination.
- Pick up your teen when it is time to come home.
- Make sure your teen always carries identification.
- Be involved in school activities so you have an opportunity to view your teen in the school setting.
- Though it may sound radical to some, I know several parents who occasionally visit school and even sit in on class. Occasionally, drop in at their work, or other activities.
- Regularly spend time one on one with your teen. Find an activity you both enjoy and listen to your teen.
- Never let down your guard.

Molesters, traffickers, and evil people are astute at what they do. They prey upon a person's weaknesses. They get into people's minds. Void of a moral or ethical compass, they bully, threaten, manipulate, and hurt their victims. They seek out the girl who needs love in her life. Who is lonely, starved for attention, naïve, and trusting. When an older boyfriend showers her with presents and sweet talk, it seems too good to be true. And it is. The trap is set and sprung.

Parents, teachers, principals, coaches, law enforcement officers, medical, and counseling professionals must listen for the child's silent cry. Look deep within the child's soul for the true answer. You may save a life. Ignoring the problem and being too cowardly to get involved only validates to the victim that they are worthless, guilty, unworthy, the one at fault. While trafficking victims are most often women, boys are targeted, too.

The following are clues that a person might be a victim of human trafficking:

- indications that they are being controlled
- bruises or other signs of physical abuse
- abrasions around the wrists, ankles, or neck
- frequent body soreness
- inability to go to another place without someone's permission
- fear
- depression
- sudden change in behavior
- sudden drop in grades
- new set of friends, particularly older ones who are unfriendly and distant to adults
- new cell phone, expensive jewelry, or other items you know their family could not afford
- frequent, unexplained absences from school
- frequently truant
- dropping out of activities they used to enjoy
- out in public without identification or money
- not knowing where they are
- chronically runs away from home
- makes reference to frequent travel to other cities, but doesn't know specifics about the location
- is hungry or malnourished
- is inappropriately dressed based on the weather conditions or surroundings
- shows signs of drug addiction
- makes reference to sexual situations that are beyond age-specific norm (a challenge these days due our highly sexual culture)
- has a boyfriend who is noticeably older
- makes reference to terminology of the commercial sex industry

Environmental signs include:
- locks on the outside of a door (as opposed to inside)
- bars on windows
- people sleeping and working in the same location, and in cramped, over crowded conditions
- sparse living conditions, generally a mattress only on the floor

These signs of sexual exploitation are not easy to see. This allows human trafficking to occur in our own neighborhoods. Be willing to care. You may save a life.

Because no one was brave enough to save me, a part of my soul died in that suburb of Detroit. No 16-year-old child should have to learn this base sense of survival.

For victims of human trafficking, the chances of survival are slim. The numbers who escape are slimmer. But the struggle doesn't end there. Recovery, healing, and becoming a productive member of society is another challenge. All victims, regardless of their age when the victimization began, how long it endured, or how violent it was, will suffer post traumatic stress disorder and depression. Many are diagnosed with borderline personality disorder. Once free, their bodies can heal, but their minds are broken. Their spirit is lost or wounded.

Recovery requires a loving, accepting, knowledgeable therapist to treat these victims. To be effective, counselors must become educated on trafficking, prostitution, and deprogramming for those that suffer from Stockholm Syndrome. In my research, I found that Cognitive Behavior Therapy yields the greatest results for helping the patient to reframe their incorrect thoughts, reconnect with themselves, and once again merge the physical with the emotional. Their body with their soul.

There is some discussion that hypno-therapy and EMDR might be of benefit due to the trauma they have suffered. But I am not entirely sure about this. It would most likely depend on the severity of the trauma. My instinct is that someone who has been repeatedly brutalized will not allow their mind to shut off. For their subconscious to release control over the psyche. From experience, neither practice has been successful because I simply could not trust enough and let go.

Successful counseling must focus on trust, security, and self love. Victims find it difficult, if not impossible, to trust others (and perhaps themselves) because they feel everyone has let them down and hurt them. Often victims are so desperate for someone special in their lives that they trust too freely – giving their trust to untrustworthy people. This perpetuates the cycle of being a victim who is victimized which reaffirms they are a victim. They will never feel safe and secure due to the trauma and the resulting drama. Being always on guard, waiting for the next blow is exhausting.

Whether unable to trust or trusting without discernment, victims find it nearly impossible to love themselves. The combination of intense guilt, shame, and being without a voice and without a name, prevents them from developing any healthy feelings of self. Unable to trust themselves, they let others make decisions for them but are consistently unhappy with the results. Their world is like a small glass box where they remain trapped, watching everyone else enjoy life.

President Bush, in his address to the General Assembly on September 23, 2003, stated, "There's a special evil in the abuse and exploitation of the most innocent and vulnerable." As a social worker, as a survivor, and as a parent, I advise you:

Sharpen your claws against wrong doing, against human suffering.

Have ears like owls, hear what the child isn't telling you.

Have eyes like a hawk so you might see all that passes before you.

Be brave like a bear and have the courage of a mother lion to save our young.

39.
Slavery in Any Era

There has been much discussion as to whether or not my story is actually a definition of human trafficking. Experts agree that, had this been caught today, it would qualify as a human trafficking case. While it could also be considered child sexual exploitation, it does meet the definition of trafficking or domestic sex trafficking of a minor. It just isn't the typical depiction of a trafficking scenario.

The word *slavery* confuses most readers. We have not heard this word used in the United States since slavery became illegal in the 1800's, and later when every citizen was granted the right to vote in the 1960's. We banished this word from our everyday language. Other than in our history books, slavery is a term used typically when referencing third world countries. When the terms *modern day slavery, sex slave*, and *white slavery* surfaced, many were taken back.

My story takes people out of their comfort zone. People doubt the validity and truth of it. As a society, we've gotten adept at excusing away things that are distasteful. The parent screaming at the child next door, or the teen girl standing on the street corner. We tell ourselves it is fine, not what we think, and everything is good. Or they must have bad parents. We don't trust our instincts, our gut feeling, as we continue on with our business. Abandoning the innocent and vulnerable.

No victim wants to be revictimized, to stand in front of an audience to tell her dark, dirty secrets, only to be questioned and shunned once again. Human trafficking was what happened to me. I didn't expect to be doubted because I don't look like what people believe the typical victim looks like.

The definition of trafficking includes words like coercion, fraud, and force. It also can include threats, and blackmail. The words *option* and *choice* are the opposite of slavery or human trafficking. If we judge that a person has an option, then it cannot be slavery. But bondage can be unseen. It can encompass psychological bondage as well as physical.

Many are quick to accuse a girl of having had other options versus having chosen a life of prostitution. To follow this reasoning, we can ask, did plantation slaves have other options in the 1700's? While owned by a master, they lived in a small home or shack, provided with a set of clothing, a bed, and food. They were beaten if they didn't do as told or work hard. For the most part they were not kept in shackles daily. Theoretically, escape was an option. But we have learned their bondage, like mine, was psychological as well as physical.

Could they have run away? Escaped? Some did. Some survived their escape but a great many did not. Is life in bondage better than life-threatening punishment or death? Escape didn't mean instant freedom. It meant their predators would hunt them, it meant they had to leave family, make their way into an unknown region, into an unknown future, usually alone, with no money, and no one to trust.

Today if a child in a third world country is kidnapped and forced to work on a plantation, do they have other options? Could the child run away? If a young woman is brought from another country to be a maid in an exclusive, rich neighborhood, yet she is faced with beatings and sexual assault, do we ask if she has other options? Could she call the police? Simply leave when the owners were away from the house?

When it comes to modern day slaves, whether forced prostitution or trafficking, we forget that they were being held in psychological bondage. Fear is a major factor, induced by coercion, force, and threats.

Twenty years ago, our society thought a woman who was a victim of domestic violence could simply walk away. Through education and awareness, we begin to understand what occurs for the woman mentally. We realize that she has to be ready to leave, and she has to feel as if she has another option that is better than what she is living through. We also have shocking statistics of women who fled domestic violence only to be stocked and killed by their abuser.

The same applies for the child of sexual abuse. It is not simple. Traffickers, pimps, violent husbands, and molesters are extremely skilled in making a person feel loved, then abusing them for their selfish pleasure, then apologizing and starting the toxic cycle over by making them feel loved again. All the while the predator assures the victim that they have no choice but to live in silence and make the best of the situation. The tactics are so insidious, that the victim believes him.

Why is it difficult for society to blame the perpetrators rather than the victim? In all my speaking engagements, no one has voiced their fury at the men who used and abused me. But plenty have laid the blame at my feet, telling me I could have chosen to escape. This revictimizes people like me. I believe this is a large contributing factor to why so many victims remain silent. I believe the public reacts this way out of their own fear. They don't want to accept that this heinous crime could happen close to home; to someone they know, to their loved ones. It is a form of denial.

40

How Could This Be?

by Dr. Jeffrey Barrows

As an OB/Gyn and health consultant on human trafficking for the Christian Medical Association, I do a lot of public speaking on the health consequences of human trafficking. Audiences frequently question how human trafficking can occur all around us and still remain hidden.

For instance, I can understand that some might question the veracity of certain aspects of Theresa's story such as the fact that she never became pregnant throughout her entire ordeal, even though she wasn't using any contraception. What non-medical people fail to realize is the vast influence emotional stress has on the reproductive system.

As an OB/Gyn, it does not surprise me to learn that Theresa never became pregnant throughout this terrible episode in her life. Severe life threatening stress would likely cause Theresa to stop ovulating (releasing an egg) on a regular basis. The process of ovulation is very intricate and very much under the control of the central nervous system. When a woman is not ovulating, she will not get pregnant.

This likely scenario is supported by the fact that Theresa has reported to me that during this difficult season in her life, she experienced long episodes where she did not have a period, and when they occurred, they were very irregular. This is typical for a woman who is not ovulating on a regular basis. Therefore, it is quite easy to attribute the fact that Theresa did not get pregnant through this time of repeated forced sexual activity because of the secondary emotional stress that was brought on by this terrible ordeal.

Beyond that, I agree that while Theresa is very fortunate that she did not incur any other sexually transmitted infections, that fact does not in any way lessen the truthfulness of her account. For instance, I just returned from Nicaragua where I was part of a medical team that screened over a hundred known prostitutes for sexually transmitted infections. Aside from a few cases of an infection known as trichomonas, we did not encounter a single case of HIV, syphilis, gonorrhea, or chlamydia among these known prostitutes.

While it is expected that the incidence of sexually transmitted infections will be greater among women who are forced into prostitution as Theresa was, it does not necessarily mean that they will automatically become infected.

Dr. Jeffrey Barrows is the founder of Gracehaven and an expert on human trafficking.

My Definition: A Poem

Do not ask why I can act so well,
For I had to in order to survive.
Do not ask how old I was when I lost my virginity,
For the age is not a reflection of having an option.
Do not ask how many men I have been with,
For I do not know the answer.
Do not ask why I can perform certain sexual acts so well,
For my practice was unwanted and vast.
Do not ask me my story,
For you really don't want to know.
Do not ask me to lie,
For I prefer the truth over lying for my survival now.
Don't ask me how I became so strong,
For you can't even imagine.

Don't ask me why I am so spiritual,
For only the angels were with me on my darkest journey.
Do not ask me how many times I was pregnant,
For only God knows how many times He removed the seeds from me.
To spare me an even harder burden.
Don't ask me if I had a choice or why I didn't run.
For what person would endure what I did if given a choice?
Do not ask me if I have been abused,
For you can not even fathom the abuse that took place.

Do not ask me what I was like when I was young,
For that person no longer exists.
Do not ask me what regrets I have in life or what I would change if I
could,
For I have no regrets about the decisions I made.
For you see,
I did what I had to do to protect my family.
I had no choices.

I became strong and found the Spirit within myself.
I became the woman I am today due to all of my experiences.
Both negative and positive.

Many will say I shouldn't allow these things to define me.
But it does.
Yet only in the positive way I permit and allow it to.

The Face of a Trafficking Victim

Years later,
I try to reassemble my heart.
Unearth what was buried.
For protection. For safety.
Pretending to have a normal life.
Just like you.

Ceaselessly, I was what they made me be.
Everyone's expectations crushing me.
Not wanting to disappoint.
Needing to please.
No matter the cost.
Or else.

Each trafficking victim experiences
the same shattered self.
Broken soul.
Regardless of the color of my skin,
the shape of my eyes,
the country I was born in,
the money I grew up with.
Despite my vices,
background,
education.
If I had two parents,
or one,
or none.
I was sold by parents
to feed a drug addiction.
Or tricked,
lured.
Hungry for love.
Kidnapped off the streets
near home.

Out for ice cream.
Or running from something worse.
Only to exchange one abuse,
one violation,
one exploitation
for another.
Our faces are different,
We endured harshness.
Hell.
Humiliation.
Violence.
Man after cruel man.
Haunted by nightmares.
Fear.
Feelings of unworthiness.

Unearthing layer
after layer.
It is time.
Tears pour as I dig deeper
and deeper.
Dangerously close to the core.
Where pain festers.
Unable to be hidden any longer.
The truth screams to be released.

Who am I?
I lost myself so long ago.
Gushing away with my blood
After the first blow to my womanhood.
The real me slipped away.
To protect myself.
Hiding.
To be found again,

years later.
When it is safe.

Time to turn hell into heaven.
Find a purpose in this evil.
I am the face of trafficking.
An age old horror,
that has reigned too long.

Raise an army.
See the reality.
Save our children.
The beautiful faces of our children.

I hear their stories.
After they hear mine.
They are young women.
And old.
Whispering their similar tale.
Finding their voice.
No longer allowing
power to sadistic captors.
We prevail.

I have had many faces.
Forced to be many people.
Finding myself
has been a long journey.
A chilling road.
I need to know that little girl again.
Bind and heal her wounds.
Nurture strength
from within.
From above.

Epilogue

While writing this book and speaking publicly, I struggled with the issue of identifying the people that did this atrocity to me. Though I believe in holding people accountable for their actions, I decided to change the names of all the people in this book. Their names are tattooed into my soul, the memories still vivid.

In addition to their names, I toiled with whether or not to identify the ethnic group which they belong to. Was this important? Did it really matter? Would there be backlash from this group? Due to the current political situation, would this affect the reader's views of this particular group?

I concluded that this is my story. What was perpetrated on me was a pivotal aspect of my life. I'm choosing to share all the facts. By educating the reader on the ethnic group as a whole, explaining the circumstances that surrounded my bondage, others can understand why and how this happened, and prevent similar atrocities.

I do not wish that anyone perceive this ethnic group as a whole as evil. *Chaldeans in Michigan* is a book that cites only the wonderful aspects to this cultural group. While the men that held me in slavery were horrible people, as well as those who brutalized me, I can not conclude that all Chaldeans are bad. There are evil people within every culture, individuals who prey upon innocent people.

There is no stereo type look to traffickers and pimps. They come from all walks of life and socio-economic backgrounds. Both men and women from all races and religions, from esteemed doctors to wealthy business owners, to plantation owners and farmers. From hoodlums from the ghetto to women that were similarly victimized themselves. They come in all forms.

As well, I ask the reader not to look poorly upon my family for not being aware of what was occurring. I was good at hiding the facts, covering, and keeping the secret. My life depended upon it. For the most part, my parents trusted me. That was born out of their love for me. They did the best they could at that point in our lives. It is over and done.

I came from a good, loving, financially secure family. We had our own dysfunctions, like most all families. My parents didn't abuse me and they weren't addicts. They provided well for me and my brothers. I wasn't in the foster care system, from a broken home, a minority, poor, or a runaway. The people that did this to me had a plan. Horrible people like this prey on young girls and exploit their weakness.

As a parent now myself, I know we strive to protect our children, develop their esteem, and encourage them to tell us when something wrong is happening to them. It is equally important to educate the world to identify people who are bullying and preying on children. As adults, as the guardians of our families and our communities, we must step forth and stop it.

My parents didn't know what was happening to me, but I am convinced that my teachers, the school security guard, and the policeman did know. Yet they did nothing. That is as equally evil and abusive as what my captors did to me.

When I began doing interviews and speaking out publicly, I struggled with whether reveal my identity. Should I change my name? Should I be anonymous and hide my face? Would this affect my career, my children's life, my family's reputation, or my safety? There were pros and cons to both sides. In the end I decided that if I was going to do this, I should do it one hundred percent. Continuing to hide only allowed those men to control my life and my freedom all these years later.

Was I afraid? Yes. But I'm more afraid that this will continue to occur in the United States as well as other countries if no one dares to speak out. If no one puts a face to the victims. If no one gives victims a voice. When this happens in the United States, the land of free, it can happen to anyone.

To allow my story to grow cold on the pages, I would be as guilty as those who had done nothing to help me. Together, we can stop modern slavery. Together, we can stand against those who bully, intimidate, and violate.

The most important message of this book is that sexual slavery can happen to anyone.

References

American Academy of Pediatrics. "Sexual Abuse." 2000

Bales, Kevin. *New Slavery*. California: ABC-CLIO, Inc. 2000.

Bush, W. President. Address to the United Nations General Assembly. September 23, 2003. Washington D.C.

Coalition Against Trafficking of Women. Retrieved on February 12, 2007 from www.catwinternation.org

Estes, Richard J. and Neil Alan Weiner. 2001. "The Commercial Sexual Exploitation of Children in the U.S., Canada and Mexico" (Philadelphia: University of Pennsylvania School of Social Work).

Johnson, Joan. *Teen Prostitution*. Franklin Watts Publishing. 1992

Knickerbocker. "Prostitution's Pernicious Reach Grows in the U.S. Christian Science Monitor, October 23, 1996.

Marshall III, Daniel. *Keep Going: The Art of Perseverance*. New York: Sterling Publishing Co., Inc. 2006

Sengstock, Mary. *Chaldeans in Michigan*. East Lansing: Michigan State University Press, 2005.

Tjaden, P. and Thoennes, N. "Prevalence, Incidence and Consequences of Violence Against Women Survey. Research in Brief." Washington D.C: U.S. Department of Justice, Office of Justice Programs. November, 1998.

U.S. Department of Justice: "Trafficking and Sex Tourism." Child Exploitation and Obscenity Section. Retrieved on January 23, 2007 from www.usdoj.gov/criminal/ceos/trafficking.html

www.city-data.com/city/BeverlyHills-Michigan.html Retrieved on November 16,2006

www.city-data.com/city/Birmingham-Michigan.html. Retrieved on November 16, 2006.

www.city-data.com/city/Southfield-Michigan.html Retrieved on November 16, 2006

Notes

[i] M. Stengstock. *Chaldeans in Michigan.* p.4

[ii] Ibid. p. 6

[iii] Ibid. p. 23

[iv] Ibid. p. 6

[v] Ibid.

[vii] Ibid. p. 14

[viii] Ibid.

[ix] Knickerbocker. Prostitutions Pernicious Reach Grows in the US. Article.

[x] Bales, K. New Slavery. P. 33

[xi] Estes, R. Commercial Sexual Exploitation of Children in the US, Canada and Mexico. 2001 Study.

[xii] Ibid.

[xiii] Johnson, J. *Teen Prostitution.* P. 12

[xiv] Ibid.

[xv] Ibid. News Bureau edition. Sept. 10, 2001

[xvi] Ibid.

[xvii] Bales, K. *New Slavery.* p. 2

[xviii] Ibid.

Get Involved

If you've been moved by Thersa's story and want to get involved in helping make slavery history, there are many organizations that are working tirelessly to end human trafficking of every kind in every country.

You can learn more about Theresa's organization Traffick Free at **TraffickFree.com** and how you can help educate and bring awareness to others in your community so innocent people do not fall into the same hopeless cycle.

Here are some other recommended organizations:
- Not for Sale (www.NotForSaleCampaign.org)
- Love146 (www.love146.org)
- Grace Haven (www.GraceHavenHouse.org)
- VCOM: Women & Chidren in Crisis (www.vineyardcollege.org)
- Polaris Project (www.PolarisProject.org)
- Free the Slaves (www.FreeTheSlaves.net)
- International Justice Mission (www.IJM.org)
- Shared Hope International (www.SharedHope.org)
- Unseen UK (www.UnseenUK.org)